ANIMAL TALK

ANIMAL TALK

**Remarkable Connections Between
Animals and the People Who
Love Them**

Joyce Grant-Smith

NIMBUS
PUBLISHING LTD

Nimbus Publishing Limited
3731 Mackintosh St, Halifax, NS B3K 5A5
(902) 455-4286 nimbus.ca

FSC

Mixed Sources
Product group from well-managed
forests, controlled sources and
recycled wood or fiber

Cert no. SW-COC-003438
www.fsc.org
©1996 Forest Stewardship Council

Printed and bound in Canada
Author photo: Les Smith
Cover and interior design: Jenn Embree

Library and Archives Canada Cataloguing in Publication

Grant-Smith, Joyce, 1956-
Animal talk : remarkable connections between animals and
the people who love them / Joyce Grant-Smith.
ISBN 978-1-55109-778-7

1. Human-animal relationships—Anecdotes. 2. Animals—Anecdotes.
I. Title.

QL791.G69 2010   590   C2010-903053-2

Canada

The Canada Council | Le Conseil des Arts
for the Arts | du Canada

NOVA SCOTIA
Tourism, Culture and Heritage

We acknowledge the financial support of the Government of Canada through the Book Publishing Industry Development Program (BPIDP) and the Canada Council, and of the Province of Nova Scotia through the Department of Tourism, Culture and Heritage for our publishing activities.

Dedicated to my very understanding husband, Les, and to Jesse and Alexis, who never had to ask, "Please, Mommy, may we have a pet?" but often said, "Oh, no, Mom, you didn't bring home *another* one?!"

Also in memory of Breezey Duchess and her gentle voice.

TABLE OF CONTENTS

Breezey Duchess and Colbi

PROLOGUE

During a miserable December night of wind and sleet, a little family of cats was dumped outside the TLC Animal Shelter. By morning, they were soaked, hungry, and nearly frozen. When I arrived to do some volunteer work, the manager of the shelter was nearly frantic. The shelter was filled to capacity. What was she going to do with these poor bedraggled kitties? I agreed to take the momma cat and her two kittens home with me. It was supposed to be for a week or two. We still have them, five years later.

As my husband, Les, and I were driving home with our cage full of felines, a name popped into my head. I glanced in the backseat at the gray tabby mother, then I turned to Les. "Joba," I said. "The mother cat is named Joba." I felt quite honoured that the mother cat trusted me enough to give me her name. My husband gave me that bemused smile he always got when I did my talking-to-animals-thing and just nodded.

We decided it would be best to quarantine the new arrivals, so we set them up in a small heated room in our garage. It wasn't the Ritz, but they were warm, fed and comfy. Joba settled onto the folded blanket we provided and her two black and white kittens huddled beside her.

That evening, when I was settling down to relax with a book, another name popped into my head. "Jasper. The shy kitten with the white splotch on his nose is Jasper," I told Les.

"Hmm," he mused. "I think Jasper is a better name for the other one. He's much more rambunctious. More a Jasper type."

"Maybe so," I said. "But it's the one with the white nose that told me."

"Okay."

The next morning at breakfast, the third name came to me. "Now that's just silly!" I exclaimed.

Les looked at me askance. "What is?"

"I just got the other kitten's name."

"You mean Jacob?" he asked.

My mouth gaped open. Then I said, "So you got it too!"

"What do you mean?" he asked. "Isn't that the name you said last night?"

"No. Last night, I told you one kitten was named Jasper. The name I just got in my head was Jacob. And you got it too! I thought it was silly because the names all start with a J. I'd never do that on purpose. It's too cutesy!"

My husband blinked slowly. "Jacob. I got it too."

He doesn't look so bemused anymore when I say the animals are talking to me.

When an acquaintance in the publishing business suggested that I knew quite a lot about animals and that I should write a book about them, I felt she had a point. My focus became to write a book showing how animals are amazing communicators. The hunt for stories was on.

It wasn't difficult to find the animals or the stories. Women in my horse community gathered at a friend's place and as we chatted, tales emerged. One tale led to another and soon great stories unfolded.

As I delved further afield, I found people really wanted to talk about their amazing experiences with animals. I contacted people through animal shelters, or I learned about possible stories on the Internet. I'd phone people, introduce myself, explain what I was writing, and their stories would pour out. We'd talk over a meal, we'd talk over coffee or we'd talk on the phone. We'd talk for hours. There was so much affection and wonder in their voices as they told about their special animal companions, it was easy to understand why they were very happy to share the stories.

This is a collection of those remarkable stories.

SEARCH
AND
RESCUE

Human beings are not the only creatures who feel compassion for someone who is lost and in despair. The stories of Skrudder and Pearl tell of animal helpers who tried their best to bring a fellow creature safely home again. Without human instruction, these animals understood what had to be done, and they set out to do it.

Skrudder

Skrudder did not seem to be a particularly remarkable horse. Standing out among his herd of Icelandics at Olga Comeau's Mandala Riding and Awareness Center near Hampton on North Mountain, Nova Scotia, he probably wouldn't catch your eye unless you were partial to pintos. He wasn't drop-dead gorgeous, and his

Skrudder, a pinto Icelandic horse, with his herd.

physique was, well, *mature*. If you got to know him, you might have learned to appreciate his kindness and patience as a steady, trusted school horse.

Sweet, steady Skrudder proved himself to be a truly amazing horse one June evening in the summer of 1999. Early on that day, Christine Riddell, a friend of Olga's, brought a high-strung, chestnut Hanoverian mare named Shushona to the riding centre. By suppertime, the mare had apparently settled into her new home. Christie turned Shushona out in a small pasture.

Shushona explored the enclosure for a while. For reasons known only to the mare, she became excited and began to gallop wildly around the pasture. Suddenly, she veered and crashed right through the fence! Fully panicked, Shushona raced off into the woods.

Christie and Olga's daughter, Nella, immediately tried to follow the mare on foot. They tracked her hoof prints along trails until they came to a logged-out clearing. They lost the mare's trail among the tree limbs that littered the ground.

Nella and Christie returned to the barn. After talking the situation over, Christie and Olga decided to search for Shushona on horseback. They picked two horses that were close to the barn. Christie chose to ride Liza, a quiet black mare, and Olga took Skrudder.

They quickly tacked up and set out. They were very concerned about Shushona. The forest was a foreign landscape to her. They were afraid she would become hopelessly lost and badly injured in the vast wooded kilometres of North Mountain.

Olga and Christie returned to the logged-out clearing and managed to pick up Sushona's trail. The mare had left the old logging roads and had headed into the bush. The going was slow as Liza and Skrudder pushed through the underbrush and wove among the trees. The sun was slipping behind the mountain. It would soon be too dark to follow any signs left by the mare.

The mosquitoes started to come out in full force as the sun slid toward the horizon. Liza, the black mare, had tender skin. She found the mosquito bites worrisome at first, and then intolerable. She was becoming frantic and wanted to return home.

They came to a small clearing. Any signs of the mare's passing seemed to have vanished. Olga dismounted, hoping to find hoof prints, broken twigs, anything that would help them track Shushona.

Olga was so intent on searching for signs of Shushona that she was only vaguely aware of Skrudder as he walked beside her. His head was very close to the ground and he was swinging his nose from side to side. At first Olga assumed he was grazing. Then she realized that he wasn't eating. He was sniffing! He tugged Olga toward one of the narrow paths that snaked through the trees. Could he be tracking the mare? Olga decided to trust her horse.

There wasn't enough room to walk beside Skrudder, the trees and underbrush were so dense. Olga detached one rein from his bridle, making a makeshift "leash," and allowed him to lead her along. Skrudder continued, nose to the ground, ears pricked forward.

Poor Liza, meanwhile, was nearly beside herself with the plague of mosquitoes. Christie finally felt it would be best to send her home. She secured the reins and stirrups so that they wouldn't become snagged in branches and she set the mare free. Liza knew the woods well; Olga and Christie were certain she would return home quickly and safely. And in fact she did just that, arriving at the barn just as full dark descended.

At the barn, Nella and a few of Olga's friends waited anxiously. When Liza returned without her rider, everyone felt a moment's panic. Upon examining the saddle and bridle, though, it became very clear that Liza hadn't thrown her rider; the rider had carefully prepared the mare to come back to the stable alone.

That raised many questions. Where were Olga and Christie? Was this a request for help? Had they found Shushona? Should a search party be organized?

The group at the barn decided that it would be best to wait a bit longer. People with flashlights thrashing in the woods, looking and calling, might send Shushona into terrified flight. Sitting tight was probably the best thing to do for the time being. Liza was unsaddled and returned to her pasture. The friends at the barn waited anxiously.

Skrudder proved himself to be a truly amazing horse.

In the dark woods, Olga and Christie followed Skrudder as he snuffled along among the trees. He did not pause or hesitate, but walked steadily on.

Suddenly, he stopped and raised his head. The two women peered forward and saw a large, dark shape silhouetted against the darker forest. The shape moved. Yes! It was Shushona!

Olga and Christie were afraid that she would spook and bolt into the trees at the sight of them. They stood uncertainly for a moment, wondering how best to approach the mare. Then Skrudder whinnied and Shushona whinnied in reply. The mare stepped forward to meet him.

Christie cautiously walked up to the mare. She gently reached out, talking softly, and clipped the lead rope onto Shushona's halter. Success! Christie and Olga smiled at each other. Now they just had to find their way home through the dark woods.

Christie decided she'd rather ride the mare out of the woods than try to lead her in the dark over the rough ground. Olga boosted Christie onto Shushona's back, then she reattached the rein to Skrudder's bridle and swung into her saddle.

She scanned the darkness. Although Olga knew the woods well, they had been weaving among the trees for some time, and she couldn't get her bearings. She again decided to trust Skrudder. Olga allowed him a loose rein and said, "Okay, let's go home."

Skrudder did not turn and retrace his steps as Olga had expected. Rather, he veered to the left. Even though Olga suspected he was going the opposite direction from home, she had faith in him and she let him pick his own way. Christie followed on Shushona.

Within moments, Skrudder stepped out onto an old logging road and turned down it. He had known exactly where he was. Unerringly, he chose every correct fork in the trail to bring them home along the easiest route.

They arrived at the barn under a star-filled sky. Christie tucked Shushona safely into a stall. Skrudder received abundant praise, treats, and a rubdown—the hero's welcome that he deserved.

A version of this story, entitled *An Icelandic Bloodhound*, first appeared in the December/January 2000 edition of Horsepower magazine.

Pearl

arni Gent has been involved with the Nova Scotia SPCA and the Humane Society for years, and she was the founder of Maritime Animal Rescue. She has saved the lives of numerous animals, and has had special relationships with many of them. This story tells how Marni got some very unexpected help one day while trying to rescue a favourite pet.

A few years ago, Marni received a call from a fellow who wanted to give away a young hen. He had bought a brood of chicks, but didn't have any previous experience in raising chickens. The

Pearl had beautiful blue-black feathers with a tinge of rust around her eyes and on her breast.

pen he'd made was inadequate and a raccoon had gotten in and destroyed all the chicks but one. That one remaining chick received a damaged wing in the attack, but she had miraculously survived.

Marni already had one chicken at home and she was quite fond of her. When she saw the wounded chick, she bonded with her right away. She took her home and helped her settle in. She decided to name her Pearl.

Pearl must have thought she'd really fallen upstairs. Her new home was a coop built on one wing of Marni's garden shed. It was insulated, with windows to let in the morning and afternoon light. There were wide windowsills with perches so the chickens could sun themselves if they so desired. The side wall, where it was darker and private, held nesting boxes. A radio tuned to CBC softly played classical music. There were two heat bulbs for days when the weather got cold and damp, and there were plenty of wood shavings for bedding. Quite a step up from the situation she had just left!

Marni liked to eat breakfast out on her back porch, and the two hens would come keep her company, one hunkered down on each side, while she ate. They were good companions.

Pearl grew up to be a beautiful hen. Her feathers were a deep blue-black, with a tinge of rust around her eyes and on her breast, and her comb was a brilliant red.

Pearl got to be very tame and trusting. She liked to sit on Marni's lap and have her feathers stroked. Pearl would sometimes even doze off while lying on Marni's lap. When Marni talked to her, she responded by gently turning her head to look at her.

Even the dogs didn't upset Pearl, which surprised Marni, considering the traumatic experience she'd had as a chick with the raccoon attack.

The chickens were often allowed to free range near the house. Wild birds were with them in the yard and in the nearby trees. There were small birds—sparrows, chickadees and blue jays—as well as larger birds, such as crows.

Marni observed how the blue jays tended to be the warning birds for the smaller species. If danger approached, the blue jays would screech and holler. Then the little birds either disappeared, flying off to a safer place, or they became motionless and virtually invisible until the danger passed. The crows tended to sound the alarm for the blue jays and other large birds.

Sometimes, the birds' warnings were for a huge fox that lived in the area. Marni had seen him a few times. She wondered if his father was a coyote; he was unusually large, and his coat was more gray than red. He wasn't as shy as most foxes, either. One time he'd even chased Marni's border collie. Not typical behaviour for a fox!

One morning, Marni was helping out with the spring clean-up, picking trash out of the roadside ditch. When she was finished, she tromped home in her rubber boots. Partway up the driveway, she heard the crows making a terrific racket in her yard. "Oh no," she thought. She remembered that she'd left the chickens outside.

She picked up her pace, fearful that her hens were in danger. Sure enough, as she entered the yard, she saw the fox nearby, poking his ears up out of the long grass. The hens had also heard the crows' warning; they were huddled under a grove of trees, as still as stones.

Marni had her border collie with her. Remembering the fox's attempt to attack once before, she took time to put the dog in the car.

When she looked up again, she was horrified to see that the fox had grabbed Pearl in his jaws. The fox turned to flee. The crows continued their cacophony, and flew after him. Marni, too, chased the fox, determined that he wasn't going to take her fa-vourite hen.

The fox lit out across a field. Marni kept losing sight of the fox in the long grass, but she could tell exactly where he was be-cause of the crows. The eight birds circled above him and kept up a constant cawing. They took turns swooping down at the fox's head to torment him.

Pearl was a large, heavy chicken. The fox couldn't carry her very far before he had to drop her and rest. Then he'd snatch her up again and run a little farther. The crows gave him no peace, attacking him again and again. Marni was crying and yelling at the fox, clomping after him in her awkward boots. The fox probably started to wonder if the chicken was worth all this commotion.

After giving chase for about ten minutes, Marni noticed that the flock of crows had split up. At the edge of the field, half of the crows landed in a tree and sat there, calling. The rest of the crows flew off, continuing to harass the fox.

Marni hesitated for a moment. Why had the crows split up? Had some of them tired of the chase? Or did they have another purpose? Curiosity, or perhaps an understanding that the crows were telling her something, made Marni rush to the base of the tree where some of the crows waited. Lying nearly hidden in the grass under the tree was Pearl. She was still alive, but badly shaken.

Marni picked Pearl up. She looked up into the tree and said, "Thank you," to the crows. The birds then took wing to join their companions in pursuit of the fox.

Marni cradled Pearl in her arms and gently carried her back to the house. Chickens do not cope well with shock, and poor Pearl's heart was not able to take the strain of the fox attack. She died in Marni's arms as they entered the dooryard.

Marni buried Pearl in the hen's favorite place, in the court-yard flower garden. Her grave lies between the house and the henhouse, under a Boxwood plant, beside the bench where she used to sit on Marni's lap.

Marni was terribly upset over losing Pearl, but she marveled at how the crows had helped her that day. Their warning call alerted her that something was very wrong, so that she arrived in the yard in time to see the fox. Their pestering slowed the fox down and marked his progress as he made a run for it with the hen, making it possible for Marni to follow him, despite his speed and his ability to disappear in the grass. When the fox finally gave up and dropped Pearl, Marni might never have found the hen if some of the crows hadn't perched in the tree above her and called Marni over to that place. Once they saw that Marni had Pearl in her arms, they were content to leave the hen in her care and join the rest of the flock to chase the fox away.

Marni wasn't sure why the crows did this for Pearl. Perhaps they saw her as a comrade, having shared the yard and the food Marni left there. Marni was very certain, though, that the crows were doing their best to save the young hen. Their behaviour was not that of animals joining in a hunt; they were acting as if they were protecting a flock member. Although the story doesn't have a happy ending for Pearl, Marni will never forget the teamwork and communication of the crows that day.

DEVOTION

Some people search their entire lives for a love that has no agenda, a love that lasts despite trials and separation. Rascal's story tells a tale of this sort of wonderful devotion.

Rascal

Rascal was a lively German shepherd–corgi mix dog, who lived with Eileen Turpin and her family in the small community of Cherry Hill.

Eileen discovered him in the window of a pet shop. He looked a lot like a small German shepherd. He was sable with some black points and a white patch on his chest. His ears stood up proudly. He was the last puppy of the litter and he looked so lonesome that she just couldn't leave him sitting there.

Eileen's children had recently watched a Walt Disney movie and decided to name him after the dog hero, Rascal. His name turned out to be quite prophetic.

Rascal was a great dog for the children. Eileen always felt that if they were with Rascal, he'd keep them safe. He had very good people instincts, and he was always happy to be with the children, doing whatever they were doing. If they came into the house covered with mud or soaking wet, so did Rascal.

He liked to play with the neighbour's children, too, especially if they were down at the beach. He loved to fetch balls or sticks for them. The children would drop him off at the end of the day as they headed to their homes for supper. He'd return with his tail wagging happily.

He was very intelligent, and a thief extraordinaire. Cookies were his biggest weakness. If there were cookies to be had, Rascal would find a way to get them. When Eileen was baking, he used to sit and watch the cookies brown through the oven window, anticipating them with great longing.

One Christmas season, a friend left a gift under their tree. Rascal couldn't take his eyes off that package. He even slept next to it at night. When Christmas morning arrived and the package was opened, it contained homemade shortbread cookies. No surprise to Rascal! The family decided that he should have them.

If someone carelessly left a cookie on the living room coffee table, Rascal perfected the skill of walking by very casually and ever-so-slowly slipping it from the table. He was slick enough that he could do this in front of everybody and not be noticed until it was too late.

Rascal became an accomplished thief around the neighbourhood too. He learned how to sneak into neighbours' houses and help himself to strings of sausages or anything else that took his fancy.

He gained real infamy when one night he managed to slip into a neighbour's smokehouse. While pulling a whole ham down off the hook, he upset the dripping pan, spilling the fat onto the fire below, and setting the smokehouse on fire. Eileen's husband was a volunteer fireman, so he was one of the men called upon to put out the blaze. It wasn't until the next morning, though, when Rascal proudly dragged his prize ham home that the Turpins realized that *he* was responsible for the fire and the missing meat. Rascal was not very popular that day!

The smokehouse owners had two purebred German shepherds; a male named Forest and a female named Zoe. Rascal became totally infatuated with Zoe. The two German shepherds loved to roam. Eileen didn't want Rascal getting into trouble, chasing deer or bothering neighbours' livestock, so she tried very hard to keep Rascal from running with them. This was impossible whenever Zoe came into heat, though. Rascal's ardour could not be squelched. Rascal and Zoe were like Romeo and Juliet. Despite being tied, confined, and even tranquilized, Rascal would find a way to be with the love of his life. Nothing could keep Rascal and Zoe apart.

The male German shepherd, Forest, was very protective of Zoe and he and Rascal absolutely hated each other. Jealousy over Zoe made them keen rivals and they had several vicious fights over her. Rascal received a terrible wound to one of his legs in one of those fights.

That didn't stop Rascal. It just made him smarter. He started to take a companion dog, a Doberman pinscher named Kaiser, with him when he went to court Zoe. The Doberman would distract Forest, and then Rascal and Zoe would slip away.

One evening shortly after Christmas, Rascal went outside and didn't come home. Eileen went to the back door time after time, calling for him. The longer he stayed away, the more anxious she became. It was a cold night and it was snowing. He should have been curled up in the house, warm and snug.

Finally, on a hunch, Eileen phoned Zoe's owners and asked if Zoe was in heat. That might explain Rascal's absence. The neighbours said that Zoe was also missing. Well, it seemed very likely that the dogs had run off together again.

Rascal arrived home around six o'clock the next morning, apparently no worse for his night out. Eileen was very relieved to see him back, safe and sound. She called the neighbours to tell them that Rascal had returned. The neighbours told her that Zoe had not. But Forest, their male German shepherd, who'd been home all night, disappeared first thing in the morning.

Over the next couple of days, Eileen and her neighbours noticed a pattern to the male dogs' behaviour. Whenever Forest came home, Rascal would disappear. Several hours later, Rascal would return and Forest would leave. Zoe did not come home.

Eileen and her neighbours surmised that the two male dogs must know where Zoe was. They tried to follow Rascal or Forest in an effort to find the missing Zoe. The male dogs tended to run off in the early morning or in the evening. These were the short, snowy days of late December. The owners hurried along behind Rascal or

Forest, but every time, the dog outdistanced them and disappeared into the bush. Zoe's whereabouts remained a mystery.

This went on for three days. Then Eileen received a phone call from a fellow who lived in Broad Cove, a village about seven kilometers away. He said that he had a trap line, which he had not checked for a few days, what with the holidays and all. When he went back out to check his traps, he found a German shepherd in one, caught by her leg. He wanted to set her free, but he couldn't get near enough to release her because another big dog was ferociously guarding her. He tried going back later on in the day, but there was a different dog with her, who also wouldn't let him near the female.

Eileen realized right away what had happened. Zoe had been snared in the trap on the night she and Rascal had run off, and since then Rascal and Forest had taken turns looking after her. They had somehow worked out shifts so that Zoe was never left alone.

When Zoe's owners went to the trap line to free her, there were bits of rabbit skin lying all around. The two male dogs had hunted rabbits for her to keep her fed while she was trapped. She had eaten snow to quench her thirst. Either Forest or Rascal had lain with her during the nights, so she didn't suffer from the cold. Except for the injury to her leg from the trap itself, Zoe was in excellent shape.

The synchronization of Rascal's and Forest's shifts was a real mystery to Eileen and her neighbours. As far as they could tell, the two male dogs did not meet one another during their vigil with Zoe. But somehow they knew whose turn it was to be with her.

What wonderful devotion they showed for Zoe! Despite their hatred for one another, they put her needs ahead of their own feelings. She was cherished by her male companions like a fair damsel in a tale of knightly chivalry. Such romance is rare indeed.

SAYING GOODBYE

nimals seem more at ease with the cycle of life than most people. Even across the barrier of death, animals reach out to one another. They may pay tribute at the passing of a companion or send a message of comfort to those left behind.

Gray

You couldn't help but notice Gray. He was a magnificent horse that reminded people of the chargers of old; you could easily imagine a knight in fully armoured regalia astride his back, ready to enter a jousting tournament. Gray was a beautiful dapple-gray, with great dark eyes in his finely formed head, and a well-crested neck. He was a big horse, standing approximately 16.3 hh (1.7 metres) at the withers, and solidly built. His breeding was Percheron, thoroughbred, and hackney cross.

Gray looked like he should be carrying a knight in full regalia on his back.

Olga Comeau, of Hampton, Nova Scotia, purchased Gray when he was a six-year-old. She fell in love with his bold bearing and his playful nature. When she first saw him at a riding camp in Lawrencetown one summer, she thought of him as her "dream horse."

Gray's owner at the time was planning a move to British Columbia within the year. Olga kept in contact with him over the next few months and let him know that if he decided to sell Gray rather than take him to British Columbia, she was interested in purchasing him. Eventually, the owner agreed to sell Gray to her. She had her dream horse.

Olga rode Gray all over the North Mountain, enjoying the many trails through the woods. She also took him to pony camps in Lawrencetown, where she taught lessons and supervised the campers. Later on, her daughter Nella competed on Gray in Pony Club events and he was used as a lesson horse for more advanced riders at Mandala Riding and Awareness Center.

For years, Gray was the undisputed boss horse of his field. The mares of his herd, Velvet and Blossom, each had her share of pony feistiness. Velvet was a black Shetland pony cross with a sweet little dished face. Blossom was a bay pony mare with some Morgan horse in her blood. They willingly respected Gray's bulk and leadership.

One day Nella bought a huge chestnut gelding for competing in cross-country. He was named The Turk. He was also 16.3hh. He was a bit lighter in stature than Gray, but he had a lot of attitude. He decided that *he* was going to be the boss of the herd.

Gray found his demotion to number two in the herd a hard thing to take. He had been king of the pasture for years, and now The Turk pushed him aside. Gray became listless and depressed.

It took a long time, but gradually he and The Turk sorted out their differences, and although The Turk remained the herd boss, he and Gray actually became good friends.

Gray's playful nature showed itself in his relationship with The Turk. If he found a large tree branch lying in the pasture, Gray would carry it in his mouth to where The Turk was standing. He would poke The Turk with the branch until The Turk whirled around and grabbed hold of the other end in his teeth. Then they would play tug-o-war with the branch. It was quite a spectacle to watch those massive animals pulling each other back and forth across the field. Occasionally, if a tree branch wasn't handy, a tire or a feed tub would suffice as their tug-o-war "rope."

Gray's zest for life came through whenever he received his ration of feed. He enjoyed it so much that he would frequently throw out a hind hoof as he ate as an expression of satisfaction. When he was fed in the barn, his hoof often connected with the stall wall, rattling the side of the barn like a thunderclap. That startled more than one visitor to the stable at feeding time!

Gray's playful side also showed itself when he was being ridden. Sometimes, just for the sheer joy of it, he would give a buck as he cantered along. There was nothing malicious about it; he was just having fun. One tended not to daydream when riding Gray.

Olga remembered once having a chance to ride Gray on the harness racetrack in Greenwood. It was so exhilarating to let the powerful horse stretch out and gallop full speed along the track. Because he thought it was so great, too, Gray gave a buck in the middle of a stride. He caught Olga completely off guard. She was unseated, and landed up on Gray's muscular neck as he continued to gallop. Fortunately he didn't put his head down or throw in another buck for good measure. If he had, Olga would have had a nasty spill. As he raced along, she was able to push herself back into the saddle and continue the exhilarating ride.

Aside from the occasional buck, Gray was a dream to ride. His canter was full of power and propulsion. His riders felt as if he could soar off, like Pegasus, as he collected his hindquarters and surged forward.

The summer that Gray was twenty-three years old, he began to lose weight, and he seemed "off." Olga called in the vet, and after blood tests it was determined that Gray had stomach cancer. Olga was heartsick.

Gray grazing in his summer pasture.

Everyone who knew Gray was devastated by the news. He was a favourite with anyone who had worked with him.

Olga felt that as long as Gray continued to be comfortable, he would remain with his herd mates. In the months to come, Gray enjoyed sunning himself on the hillside in his pasture and basking in the attention that his many friends gave him. His weight dropped, but the light in his eyes and his zest for life shone on for some time.

A year after the vet's diagnosis, he succumbed to his illness. Olga put Gray's herd mates in the barn. She did not want the other horses to have to watch his death or his burial. The veterinarian eased Gray quietly from this life, sparing him any more pain and suffering.

Gray was buried on the hilltop where he'd always loved to stand in the sunshine.

Once the backhoe left, Olga sadly turned the herd back out into their field. Then, with tears streaming down her cheeks, she witnessed the most astonishing thing.

The horses, lead by The Turk, slowly walked in a single file procession to Gray's grave. They calmly formed a circle around the gravesite, all facing the disturbed earth. The horses lowered their heads, their noses almost touching the ground. They stood like that—quiet, motionless, and reverent—for about half an hour. Then, like bereaved family members leaving a cemetery, they slowly moved off and began to graze. The horses who had shared their pasture and their lives with Gray had paid homage to their friend and companion.

Barney

Barbara Claussen, a tall, attractive woman with a soft German accent and a ready laugh, lives in Bridgewater, Nova Scotia. Besides running a real estate business with her husband, Tony, Barbara runs a horse rescue farm. She has two donkeys and several Pregnant Mare Urine horses (or PMU horses), young horses that are the by-products of farms where mares are impregnated to produce estrogen for birth control pills. Some of these farms did not treat their horses well, cutting costs on care to try and maximize profits, and Barbara attempts to place these horses in caring homes. She and Tony have a variety of cats and dogs on their farm as well.

Barney had a darling black nose and button eyes.

One little dog who was very dear to Barbara was a black Scottish terrier named Barney. Barbara had purchased Barney from a breeder in Berlin for her parents. Scotties are known to be good companions for seniors since they are calm and quiet, which was why she thought he'd be a good choice for them. Her mother loved Barney right away, but her father decided that he didn't want a dog. So when Barbara moved to Nova Scotia, she brought Barney with her.

Besides having a darling little black nose and dark button eyes fringed with a mop of hair, Barney had an endearing personality. He loved the other dogs and cats on the farm. He was always gentle and he seemed to have a great respect for life.

One day, he found a chicken's egg. He knew it was something special; he gingerly picked it up in his mouth and set it carefully into Barbara's waiting hand, as if he were giving her a great gift. What a spiritually aware soul Barney was to realize that an egg held the precious promise of life!

Barney loved to play with balls, even huge ones.

Barbara remembered that Tony once brought home a toy wind-up mouse for the cats to play with. Tony wound it up and sent it scooting across the floor. Barney went after it. At first, Barbara and Tony thought he just wanted to play with it, like the cats. But when Barney caught up with the toy, he tenderly took it in his mouth and carried it over to his bed. He set it down, nudged it with his nose, as if to reassure it that he would keep it safe, and settled down beside it.

Barney was pretty laid back. He loved to lie in the middle of the real estate office floor, flat on his back, with his feet in the air. He had all the confidence in the world that the nine people who worked there would just walk around him. One day, as a joke, one employee made an "Out of Order" sign and placed it on

Barney's up-turned tummy. It didn't faze him a bit. He remained happily sleeping, sign and all.

Whenever Barney got hungry and he wanted to be fed, he very politely nudged Barbara with his nose, as if to say, "If you wouldn't mind, I could use a little bite of something to eat."

The only thing that would get Barney stirred up was a ball. He loved to play fetch with smaller balls. He raced after them with pure, unbridled joy. He also loved to roll around a large buoy, moored to a tree, pushing it with his head. The ball was several times larger than he was, but that didn't matter to Barney. He'd growl and attack it like he was a Great Dane going in for the kill.

Barney would sometimes bury his smaller balls so nobody else would find them. At the end of the day, he would collect and arrange his balls in bed with him so he could have them curled up next to him as he slept.

Going for walks was just too boring without a ball to take along. He always had one with him. Balls were his passion.

One fine summer day Barney met with trouble. Barbara's dogs had been trained to stay out of the pastures. This was for their own good. Donkeys are very territorial, and generally not friendly toward dogs.

Barney wandered into the apple orchard. That area was used as pasture only occasionally. The Scottie didn't realize that one of the donkeys was nearby. Barney discovered a bone under an old outbuilding in the orchard, and he was so engrossed with digging for it that he didn't hear the donkey approaching.

Barbara found Barney later, barely alive, with blood dripping from his mouth. She rushed him to the vet, fearing that even if he lived, he would be paralyzed. Amazingly, Barney survived the attack. With loving care, he made a slow but full recovery. Barbara was greatly relieved that he was going to be all right.

But then, a month later, he developed a limp. His front leg was x-rayed and the test revealed deterioration of the shoulder bone. The area that had been injured by the donkey attack had developed bone cancer.

The vet's report was an awful blow to Barbara. She was determined to give Barney as long and as happy a life as she possibly could.

Finally, in February, the pain from the cancer became overwhelming. At only eight and a half years of age, at what should have been his prime, sweet Barney no longer enjoyed life. Barbara and Tony knew they had to let him go and they had the vet put him down.

They buried Barney on the west side of their house, where he'd liked to sit and watch visitors arrive in the parking area. He'd liked to meditate there in the evenings as the sun went down, too, especially if the sky was particularly red. The spot overlooked the pond where he'd liked to hunt for frogs. They marked his grave with a large white granite stone with a metal Scottish terrier standing on the rock.

Barbara was distraught over Barney's loss. The day he was put down dragged on and on. She and Tony took their other dogs for a long walk.

On the night of Barney's death, while she was doing the barn chores, Barbara's heart was unbearably heavy. As she started back to the house, distraught and weeping, she looked up at the sky and wished for a sign from Barney. She desperately wanted to know that he had been ready to leave this world, that he was all right where he was, and that he was at peace. "I'd like to see a shining, falling star," she thought. That would have been a fitting sign from her dear Barney. Since the night was overcast, there was no chance of seeing that sort of sign.

Barbara went into the house to change out of her barn clothes, weighed down with grief, and was shocked by a large orange ball whizzing at her. It ricocheted around the room like a giant pinball.

Once she got over her surprise, Barbara realized that the stray cat they had rescued from starvation a couple of months previously had found a basketball and was playing madly with it. The ball was flying around the room, banging into furniture and bouncing off the patio doors.

The cat was a brown and black tiger with white paws, chest, and tip on her tail. Tony had named her Angel, although Barbara had never been able to figure out why he'd picked that name for her. Angel had never touched the basketball before. Now here she was, acting absolutely crazy over it.

Barbara realized she was receiving her sign from Barney. It wasn't a shining star, but what could be a clearer message from Barney than a ball, his most prized possession, sent whizzing at her by an "Angel"? Barbara was comforted to know that wherever Barney was, he was enjoying himself.

RAISING BABIES

When someone makes a special connection with a pet, it is a marvellous occurrence. When a person is able to make a connection with a wild animal, it is a moment to be cherished. That extra leap of faith, made between a creature of the forest and a human being, can be almost magical.

Emma and Ede

Marianne Leblanc, a pleasant young woman with cinnamon-coloured hair and smiling eyes, was working at the Upper Clements Wildlife Park, near Annapolis Royal, during the summer of 2003. A phone call came to the park office from Dr. David MacHattie, DVM. A woman and her daughter had been walking along the highway and had found a whitetail fawn in the ditch. They'd brought it to his clinic. Would the wildlife park take it?

Through the Department of Natural Resources, Marianne learned that the fawn was an orphan; a car had killed her mother. Marianne readily accepted the challenge of trying to raise the fawn.

The baby deer, who Marianne named Emma, was not much larger than a cat. Emma's reddish-brown back was mottled with white spots. Her ears and dark eyes seemed enormous.

Marianne was given careful instructions for the fawn's care and feeding. She realized that she would have to take the baby home with her each night, as Emma had to be fed every four hours, like any infant.

The first evening, Marianne placed Emma in a TV box lined with blankets, and set her in the sun porch where it

Emma was not much bigger than a cat when Marianne first started to care for her.

Marianne fed Emma from a bottle every four hours.

was cool and quiet. Marianne thought Emma might feel more at home there.

Emma didn't agree. She cried and cried, a high-pitched honking sound. Marianne thought if she left Emma for a while, the fawn would eventually quiet down and sleep. However, the pitiful crying continued.

When she got ready for bed, Marianne took the fawn up to her room, and set the TV box up in a corner. Maybe the baby would sleep there.

No such luck. Again, Emma cried and cried. Marianne listened from her bed for what seemed like hours. She finally took one of the blankets from the box, set it on the floor next to her bed, and lay the fawn on it. Marianne went hopefully back to bed.

Emma stood up, looked Marianne in the eye, and began to cry again.

Marianne sighed, got out of bed, and sat on the floor with the fawn. Perhaps the baby was hungry. Marianne went to the kitchen to prepare a bottle for her. Emma stood in the bedroom doorway, crying all the while Marianne was in the kitchen. Marianne returned to the bedroom, fed the fawn, and groomed her with a warm washcloth, mimicking the washing tongue of a doe.

Emma was still not content. Once her meal was over, she continued to bleat in that heart-wrenching way. At last, Marianne took a pillow off her bed and lay down on the blanket on the floor. Emma tiptoed over to her. She rested her head on Marianne's chest, just under her chin, and tucked her body up close to her. Snug and warm against Marianne, Emma was content and she slept.

Marianne was wakened four hours later by the fawn licking her forehead. It was time for her next feeding.

Emma bonded to Marianne that quickly. She travelled back and forth with Marianne from her home to the wildlife park every day so she could be fed and groomed regularly.

Two days after Emma came into Marianne's care, a second fawn was brought to the park. Just like Emma, she was orphaned when a car struck the doe. Marianne decided to adopt this fawn as well and she named her Ede. Ede was much weaker than Emma had been when she came to Marianne, but with loving care, she gained strength. Now Marianne had two babies to feed and groom and watch over!

At first, Emma was a little jealous of the new arrival. She didn't want to share Marianne. She demanded to be fed, climbing

Now Marianne had two babies to feed and watch over!

all over Marianne, if her bottle wasn't offered at the same time that Ede's was.

At least the fawns kept each other company at night so that Marianne no longer had to sleep on a blanket on the floor.

After a month, a holding pen was set up for the fawns at the park, and as they grew, they were moved to a pen that was close to the other whitetail deer so that they could be introduced to the herd.

That same summer, a huge Clydesdale horse named Champ and his strange companion, a miniature donkey named Ben, moved into the park. They quickly settled in at their new home and park visitors enjoyed viewing the Mutt and Jeff pair.

Their small pasture soon became badly grazed over, though, so it was decided that the horse and donkey could be moved into the adult whitetail deer enclosure, where there was plenty of grass and lots of room. The day of the move, everything seemed to go well. The deer simply moved to the far end of the pasture, away from the horse and donkey, and all the animals grazed peacefully.

Eventually, Champ and Ben noticed Emma and Ede's pen. They became curious and sauntered over to check it out. Upon seeing the horse and donkey, the fawns went into panicked flight. They had no idea what those strange creatures were and they repeatedly dashed themselves against the wire walls of their enclosure in a vain attempt to get away. Marianne, who was working at admissions at the time, was called to help. When Marianne got to Emma and Ede, their faces were cut and bleeding from the wire and they were frantic.

The deer were always glad to see Marianne, and nuzzled her affectionately.

Marianne stepped into the fawns' pen and spoke soothingly to them. They immediately came to Marianne and let her stroke them. Once she had Emma and Ede calmed down, Marianne walked over to Champ and Ben and patted them and talked to them. The fawns watched for a moment with wide eyes. Then they followed Marianne over to the strange animals. They touched noses with the horse and donkey and began to act like they were the best of friends. It was apparent that if Marianne thought there was no danger, then it was all right. They trusted her implicitly.

When they were old enough, Emma and Ede joined the herd of whitetail deer at the wildlife park and they lived there until the park closed, delighting visitors by eating corn from their hands and allowing themselves to be patted. And of course, they always loved to see Marianne coming to feed them, nuzzling her affectionately.

The Pride

Gail and Ron Rogerson didn't set out to create a zoo in Aylesford, Nova Scotia. However, as they acquired interesting and exotic animals on their farm, more and more people became curious and dropped in to visit. It got to the point where the Rogersons felt they would either have to open the farm to the public or move. That was the beginning of the Oaklawn Farm Zoo.

They have had many wonderful animals at the zoo over the years, and it's obvious that they care about them all. The following story tells how Gail has bonded in an extraordinary way with their pride of lions.

One of the most astonishing things to watch at Oaklawn Farm Zoo is Gail feeding the pride. She enters their compound with a wheelbarrow full of meat and calmly feeds the huge cats, passing out hunks of meat to them as if she were passing plates of food out to a group of children.

Gail can be seen in the lion enclosure during the day, cleaning up droppings or mowing the grass. She often pauses in her

Gail Rogerson feeding the lions. Rutledge has his meal. Tawny is selecting hers from the wheelbarrow.

chores to pat a maned head or scratch an upturned tummy. It looks for all the world like she's dealing with a group of house-cats, except that these cats weigh well over three hundred pounds.

Gail and Ron got their first pair of lions, Leo and Cleo, in the early 1980s. The big cats had their first litter of three cubs in 1986. Gail and Ron didn't realize that Cleo wasn't able to nurse the young ones properly until three days had passed. Two of the cubs didn't survive, but they were able to save one male. They named him Lambert.

Lambert was brought into the house to live with Gail and Ron. He was bottle-fed, and he became a foster baby to the family bulldog, Maggie. He slept in Gail and Ron's bed with them, along with their dogs. Gail and Ron put two double beds together to make a super-sized bed so they wouldn't end up on the floor!

Each morning, when the alarm clock made that tiny clicking noise that clocks do just before the alarm goes off, Lambert rolled on top of Gail and grabbed her thumb in his mouth and began to suck on it. Gail took to wearing Band-Aids to protect her thumbs when she went to bed at night. Lions have very rough tongues.

When Lambert was old enough to go outside, he followed Gail and the dogs around in the yard. Imagine being a visitor to the zoo and seeing a woman walking along with three small dogs and a lion cub trailing happily behind her. Not something you see every day.

Lambert lived in the house until he was a very large, fifteen-month-old cat. Later he was introduced to Suzi, the tiger. In 1992, he started to co-habit with younger siblings and the next year he became head of a pride of nine lions in a one-acre compound. Gail has always been very fond of her first adopted cub; he holds a special place in her heart. She said of him, "He was my best lion ever."

Gail house-reared all the lion cubs born on the farm. She did this for a couple of reasons. One was to ensure their survival. The lioness had trouble nursing her young, and so the babies had to be bottle-fed. The other reason was just as important. Gail explained, "Animals that are going to be living forever in zoos—who are born in zoos—are much happier if they are handled and are accustomed to people."

So over the years, Gail has often had a little parade of dogs and lion cubs following her about the farm.

To get used to living outside, and to be reintroduced to the pride, the cubs spent time in the barrier area—the fenced-in space just outside the lion enclosure that keeps people at a respectful distance from the big cats. One day, two young cats, named Kiaya and Aslan, managed to get the barrier area door unlatched and they were running loose within the zoo. They headed back to the house. Ron saw them in the yard and thought they should be put back inside, so he opened the back door and let them into the kitchen.

Unknown to Ron, there was a large bowl of dressed rabbits, ready for the freezer, on the kitchen table. By the time Gail got back into the house, the two cubs were happily enjoying "a tasty treat up on the bed."

Explaining her rapport with the big cats, Gail said, "Probably one of the reasons I get along with the lions so well is because I'm part of the pride. But I'm not a threat in any way...a female who is bringing home a kill." There is complete mutual trust between Gail and the cats.

She explained, "It's very important when working with the big cats that you always stand your ground, you're consistent, you have good common sense and know when *not* to go in. And you know how you get that rush of adrenaline when you're frightened by something, or startled or whatever? If you have that—if you get that feeling when you're in with the cats—then you should never go in with big cats."

Gail also uses body language and her knowledge of cat behavioor when she's with them. She does not get between two cats

Gail walks with Rutledge, who holds the Guinness world record for largest lion in captivity at 807 pounds.

that are vying for a piece of meat. She doesn't step between a male cat and a female that he wants to guard.

Gail believes that it would be unsafe for any man to walk into the lion compound, even her husband. Though the cubs lived in the house with Gail and Ron, his maleness could trigger aggression in the adult cats. Testosterone seems to be an inherent challenge with many animals.

A film crew from Australia came to Oaklawn Farm Zoo in June 1991 to make a documentary about the lions for the Discovery Channel. They drove through the barrier area with their equipment and set up their cameras just outside the gate to the lions' enclosure so they could get shots without the interference of the wire. There were nine lions in the compound at that time. The photographer really wanted to get some great shots and he asked Gail if he could move just two feet inside the enclosure to film. Gail said that he could try it and see. The photographer quietly lifted the camera equipment into the compound.

The instant he stepped inside, Teeka, one of the females, flattened her ears against her head and lowered her body. Gail warned the photographer to get back outside the compound immediately, which he did. He had encroached upon the lioness's territory.

Lionesses are the core of any pride. In the wild, they are the best hunters and the social leaders. The males protect the young while the females are off hunting. When a lioness brings a kill back to the pride, the dominant male eats first, followed by the matriarch. Then in order of strength, the rest of the pride eats. In this way, the strongest survive. Old, infirm lions tend to be cast off by the pride.

Gail had to be careful to establish behaviours with the cats when they were still very young. "However you treat an animal when it's young, is the behavior they'll expect when they get older. So you never encourage play with youngsters. You tolerate it, but you never encourage it." Play may seem harmless when they are the size of housecats, but they soon grow to weigh several hundred pounds, and then it becomes very serious.

The relationship between two of Gail's and Ron's dogs and some lion cubs illustrated this. One female pug named Won Ton was very good with the cubs. She licked and cared for them, but if they started to get out of line with her, she disciplined them right away. She didn't allow any foolishness from them, so when they got larger they still respected her and she felt safe around them. Another pug, Bugga, also liked the cubs, but she played with them. They'd chase each other around the kitchen and romp together. That was fine when the cubs were tiny and awkward. But when the cubs gained weight and became agile, it wasn't any fun for Bugga any more. She got so that she was terrified of the young lions, and she wouldn't go near them. A human handler would not want to make the same mistake that Bugga had made. It would be disastrous.

There are jaguars, leopards, cougars and other large cats at the zoo. Gail feeds and tends all of them. She has hand-raised those born on the farm whose mothers couldn't care for them. All the young have been handled and have learned to trust her.

She has a unique relationship with these regal, magnificent cats. Very few people could do what she does. A combination of animal savvy, confidence, and caring give Gail the ability to meet these cats face to face.

HEROES

Heroes come in many guises, and sometimes they have four feet and furry faces. An animal's act of heroism may be motivated by its devotion to its human companion. Its primary concern can be for its special person to be safe and well.

Indiana Jones

Christina (Chris) and Larry Stevens and their two sons, Justin and Devan, had wanted a Weimaraner dog for quite a while, so they were very pleased when the breeder told them a puppy was available. They decided to name the sleek, sandy coloured pup Indiana Jones, after a favourite movie character. Little did they know that the new addition to their family would live up to his name and become a hero.

Indiana Jones lived up to his name and became a hero.

Indy was an energetic, high-strung young dog. He was always looking for attention, always on the go, and always underfoot. If Chris was working around the house and turned suddenly, she'd trip over him because he was always on her heels. If Indy felt he was being ignored, he'd bark till he got somebody's attention. He was good with the boys, though, and loved to play with them outside.

Indy was an intelligent dog and he found interesting ways to amuse himself. One of his tricks was to take glasses or bowls off the ceramic kitchen counter and carry them into the living room. He never spilled the contents or broke a bowl, which was amazing considering that all the floors were hardwood.

One Friday in July 2002, Chris and Larry invited another couple, who also had two boys, over for a bonfire. The adults sat on the veranda outside their ranch-style house, enjoying the pleasant summer evening while the boys played. A citronella candle kept the pesky mosquitoes away.

They were rather late getting to bed, so Chris wasn't too happy when around three o'clock in the morning, Indy woke her up. He was pacing back and forth on the hardwood floors, his nails clicking as he walked. Like most young mothers, Chris was a light sleeper. The click, click, click of his toenails kept her from falling back to sleep.

Then Indy came over to the bed and nudged Chris with his nose. She tried to push him away, but he just kept coming back. Then he started to whine. Chris began to feel cross with Indy. Why wouldn't he just settle down and let her sleep?

Finally, Chris grumbled to Larry, "Shut the dog up."

Larry got up to see what was the matter with Indy. Maybe he had to go out.

The glow through the living room windows didn't alarm Larry at first; he thought it was just the lights from the nearby pit where dump trucks got fill. But as he reached the front room, Larry realized that the glow came from their veranda. It was on fire! He called to Chris, "The house is on fire! Get the kids out!"

Larry was a firefighter; the house was equipped with fire alarms and smoke detectors. None of these had gone off. Perhaps the fire hadn't spread very far. He grabbed a housecoat and went outside to see if he could douse the flames.

Chris sprang out of bed. The boys' bedrooms were at the front of their house, next to the veranda. Indy was right at her side as she rushed into her youngest son's room. She grabbed four-year-old Devan out of bed and tucked him under her arm like a linebacker with a football.

Indy remained glued to her side as she tore into eight-year-old Justin's room. The room was filled with an eerie, flickering light from the flames on the veranda. Devan was still tucked under one arm, so with her free hand, Chris pulled Justin out of bed. She didn't take the time to try to wake him. She simply dragged him by one arm from the room. She had just hauled him out through the bedroom doorway when the window blew in, showering his room with glass and flames.

Indiana Jones, who had up until that moment been pressed against Chris's leg, stepped ahead of her. Chris sensed that the dog felt the need to take the lead, and she unhesitatingly followed him. Although the front door was a closer exit, Indy led Chris and the boys toward the back door. Chris didn't question. She followed the eleven-month-old pup as he calmly took them out of the burning house.

Chris remembers hurrying past the laundry room and seeing a basket of clean clothes sitting there. She didn't dare take the time to stop and grab it. Chris remained right behind Indy, with her two boys tucked under her arms, as the dog lead them up the driveway to safety.

Later, Chris learned that the electrical wires leading into the house had burned off. They were still live, snaking wildly around the front door. If she and the boys had chosen to leave by that route, they could have been electrocuted. Indy saved their lives by leading them out of the burning house by the back door.

Larry joined his family by the roadside. Through the sirens, the growing crowd, the fire trucks, and the confusion, Indy remained by Chris's side. He wore no leash. He felt it was his job to guard his family and he remained steadfast.

The house was soon engulfed in flames. The Stevens could do nothing but watch helplessly as their home, and everything in it, was destroyed. Their travel trailer, car, van and ATV, all parked by the house, went up in flames. Numb with shock, they realized that they had nothing left but the pyjamas they wore and the robe Larry had grabbed on the way out of the bedroom. Their clothes, wallets, documents, furniture—everything—were gone.

The fire marshal later told the Stevens that the fire was likely started by a citronella candle, sitting on the patio table on the veranda. It ignited the siding on the house. The fire quickly ate up the siding and into the roof, and from there it spread through the ceiling. Not much smoke entered the house, so the smoke detectors didn't go off. The fire burned the electrical wires off the house soon after it started and so the fire alarm had not worked.

If Indiana Jones hadn't sensed the danger and awakened the family, they wouldn't have realized the house was on fire until it was too late. Because he alerted them, and then stayed calm and guided them outside, they got out alive.

Indy dealt with some trauma following his courageous role during the fire. He required a veterinarian's care to help settle him after that stressful night. His bravery was enormous and selfless, especially when one takes into account his high-strung personality.

Ency: The Little Mother

Wendy and Bill Knowlton moved from Nova Scotia to Ontario in 1998 in search of job opportunities.

They both enjoyed wrestling, and so they spent a lot of time working out at the Regency boxing gym in Hamilton, Ontario. One day at the gym, they discovered two bedraggled kittens. No one wanted the poor abandoned babies, so Wendy and Bill took them home.

They named the kittens Reg and Ency, after the gym where they were found. Ency, a gray and white tabby female, was very maternal. She often grabbed her dark tabby brother and held him down to give his ears a thorough washing. Reg didn't really appreciate this devoted care, and struggled to get away, but that just made Ency more determined.

Ency showed her motherly instincts toward Wendy and Bill's baby daughter as well. Whenever little Julia cried, Ency immediately raced to her. She rubbed against Julia and purred to soothe her. When Wendy and Bill took too long to get to the baby when she was distressed, Ency would turn and give them a reproachful look. It was a bit disconcerting to have their parenting skills questioned by a cat, but they felt the bond between Julia and Ency was very special. They called Ency their "little mother."

Ency, a gray and white tabby cat, was like a little mother to baby Julia.

Wendy and Bill moved back to Halifax in the summer of 2002. They found jobs, a nice apartment, and a reliable babysitter for Julia. They were happy to be home in Nova Scotia, and things seemed to be going well.

Bill and Wendy were both on the night shift at work. Usually, once the babysitter got Julia down to sleep for the night, she would have a nap since Wendy and Bill didn't finish their shift until after midnight. But one night Ency would not let the babysitter sleep. The cat prowled the apartment like a tigress, meowing and pacing from the couch where the babysitter lay to Julia's bed and back again. She jumped onto the babysitter and glared into her eyes, then paced again. At first, the babysitter was annoyed. What had gotten into that darned cat anyway? Then she became concerned. Finally the babysitter got up to see what Ency was so worked up about.

Just as she reached Julia's bed, the child began to cough in terrible, racking spasms. Julia couldn't catch her breath. Her face paled to a ghastly transparent gray. She was choking to death. In a panic, the babysitter snatched Julia up from the bed and clutched the child to her shoulder. The movement seemed to help Julia gasp in a little air. Her face turned pink. She continued to cough—a terrible, hollow, rasping sound—but at least she was breathing.

The babysitter phoned Wendy and Bill at work and they all rushed to the hospital. After examining Julia, the doctor told them that she was a very sick little girl. She had whooping cough!

Thank goodness for the "little mother." Ency, who was so sensitive to Julia's needs, felt the difference in the child's breathing and could tell she was in danger. Julia might very well have suffocated if Ency hadn't alerted the babysitter. Just a few seconds' delay might have been the difference between life and death.

Roy

Let your mind go back to a time when horses and hands did all the work on small Nova Scotia farms. Go back about fifty years to a tiny rural community called Port Wade, near Annapolis Royal.

When Roy wasn't working the fields he often had several small children on his back, enjoying a ride.

severe epilepsy. In those days, the disorder was not well understood and medication was not available to control it. His seizures came upon him suddenly and they were violent. Working with cattle and farming equipment was a risky proposition for Burton. There weren't many opportunities in those days for someone with epilepsy, though, as it was seen as a disability, so taking over the family farm was the work that was available to him.

One of the younger Holmes children, usually Dorothy, tried to stay nearby while Burton worked. Dorothy's job was to run to get help if Burton started to have a seizure. She remembers carrying a spoon around in her pocket; it was common practice in those days to slip a spoon into the mouth of an epileptic during a seizure to keep him from biting his tongue.

Dorothy got so that she was able to tell when her brother was about to have a seizure. She said his eyes would get glassy and he'd kind of stare off into space. Then she'd try to make sure Burton was in a safe place before the seizure overcame him.

Occasionally, Burton was on his own when a seizure hit. This occurred one summer day when he was in the field, mowing hay. Roy was pulling the mower while Burton sat on the machine, above the cutting blade, driving the horse. Without warning, Burton's body began to contort uncontrollably.

Such erratic movements could spook a horse, sending it into panicked flight. Burton could have been thrown onto the cutting blade and been torn to pieces. Fortunately, Roy was not just any horse. When he felt Burton losing control, Roy stopped dead still. He did not move until Burton came out of his seizure and was recovered enough to continue with the mowing.

Dorothy remembers her mother standing in the kitchen window on winter days when Burton went to the barn alone to do the evening chores. She would check the clock and keep watch for his lantern light coming across the road from the barn. If he seemed to be taking too long, she would send one of the other children down to the barn to see if he was all right.

The animals were kept in straight stalls, tied up one beside the other. The steer that was tied next to Roy could be an ugly character. He would just as soon kick someone as look at him. Dorothy remembers that everyone had to watch out for that steer for fear of being hurt.

One night when Burton was working in the barn alone, he happened to be stepping between Roy and that steer when a seizure hit him. His limbs convulsed as he went down onto the barn floor, right next to the rogue steer. Burton's strange movements sent the steer into a mad frenzy, and it tried to crush Burton. Burton was in danger of being trampled to death as he lay helplessly on the floor.

Fortunately for Burton, Roy knew what to do. Many other horses would have panicked over the steer's aggression, adding their own stamping hooves to the deadly confusion. Not Roy. He carefully moved toward the steer, placing himself directly over Burton's wracked body. He then planted his huge hooves around Burton. He stood motionless, protecting his human companion with legs like stone pillars, as the agitated steer lunged and snorted beside him.

When Burton eventually regained consciousness, he found himself underneath his horse, safe from harm. He was able to roll out from under Roy and resume his chores. Dorothy believes if it weren't for Roy, the steer would have killed her brother that day.

Roy not only remained calm when Burton needed that from him, but he understood when his friend had to have protection and he willingly and selflessly provided it.

THERAPY DOGS

Winston Churchill once said, "There is something about the outside of a horse that is good for the inside of a man." More and more people are recognizing the tremendous therapeutic facility of other animals. This chapter tells of dogs who provide special therapy for seniors and for youngsters.

Jenna and Brook

When Wendy Cook bought and began to show Brook, a chocolate Labrador retriever, and Jenna, a black Labrador retriever, she thought she'd like to do something more with them than just take them to shows. While competing at one dog show, she saw the St. John Ambulance therapy dogs, and she became interested in their work. These therapy dogs visit with people who are in palliative, acute, chronic, or long-term care, or in retirement settings. She wondered if Jenna and Brook had the qualities needed to become therapy dogs.

In January 2005, Wendy enrolled both dogs in the St. John Ambulance Therapy Dog program. Her mother joined her so that both women and dogs could become certified. Jenna was two years old and Brook was three.

Wendy was a bit worried that Jenna would find it difficult since she was a rather shy dog. The training was extensive. The dogs had to learn to be comfortable around wheelchairs and walkers. They couldn't be afraid of lab coats (often associated with vets), or strange, sudden noises. They had to be willing to have several strangers touch them while their handler was not available to reassure them.

However, both Brook and Jenna passed the certification and were ready to begin work in the two nursing homes in the Annapolis Royal area. Wendy arranged to have the dogs go into each of the homes once a week.

Wendy had Brook bred shortly after the chocolate lab became St. John Ambulance certified. Brook had nine puppies in the spring, and so Jenna did all the nursing home visits while Brook was on maternity leave. Even though she had been the shyer of the two dogs, Jenna thrived on the job and the more she did it, the better she became.

Jenna settled into her working dog mode whenever Wendy brought out the special St. John Ambulance collar, identity tag, leash, and treat bag. She was excited to go, and obviously happy to do her rounds. She tugged Wendy into the nursing home rooms where she knew the residents would welcome her.

Although Jenna loved to visit the residents, she was very careful. She never jumped up on them and she took treats from their frail fingers very gently. Jenna was always happy to see the lunch cart come around while she was visiting; she knew the residents would share lots of goodies with her. One night she enjoyed several gingersnaps as she went from room to room.

The Labrador retriever was a big hit with the residents. When Jenna walked into a room, the residents' faces lit up like they were seeing an old friend. Many of them exclaimed that "their dog" had come for a visit. Wendy chuckled that they never said that Wendy Cook had come to visit, and brought the dog. It was the dog who was the visitor. Wendy was often ignored. Jenna was the focus of attention.

Some residents couldn't remember the dog's name from week to week, but they were pleased to see her just the same. They stroked her ears and told her what a beautiful dog she was.

One resident at the North Hills Nursing Home liked to have Jenna jump onto the bed with him. She was happy to oblige, but was always very careful not to land on top of him as she hopped up.

Brook and Jenna made a welcome break in the residents' day when they visited. For some residents, though, the dogs touched them in a more profound way.

An elderly gentleman at North Hills couldn't keep his hands steady; his limbs shook uncontrollably. When Jenna came to visit him, he loved to stroke her silky ears. She sat quietly by his wheelchair and let him run his quaking hands over her head. Wendy said that after a few moments, she could see his hands become gradually steadier. The jittery shaking eased, and a look of peace and contentment came over his face.

One woman at the same nursing home was very uncommunicative. She hardly ever spoke or acknowledged other people. She liked it when Brook came to visit, though. Imagine how delighted the staff was when one day the woman surprised everyone by exclaiming, "Oh, my dog's here!" The visits from the dogs continued to help the woman's communication so that eventually she would walk the dogs along the nursing home corridor, with Wendy's help, and sing to the dogs. She missed Brook when she was home with her puppies, and would ask for "her brown dog."

Another woman sat in the common room at North Hills one evening and talked to Jenna and Wendy for about forty-five minutes, discussing dogs and her family. Later, when Wendy asked a staff member who the woman was, she was surprised to learn that she was a resident. Wendy had assumed that she was a visiting family member or a staff member of the facility. In fact, she was told that the woman was a resident who usually stayed in her room because she didn't respond well to anyone, and was very difficult to work with. She would even throw her food trays at staff members. Wendy was amazed. They'd had a lovely conversation.

The puppies were an exciting topic. The residents asked about them, and wanted to see them. Wendy made sure that a couple of the pups visited the nursing homes before they went to their new families, so that the residents could enjoy them.

Brook and Jenna touched the lives of so many seniors. Through their visits they brought joy, comfort, and companionship to the nursing home residents. Wendy Cook felt that she and her dogs were giving something back to their community.

Arthur and R.E.A.D.

The youngster sat down with the speckled English setter next to him. The nice, quiet man sat on the other side of the dog. The boy selected a book from the stack the man had brought. He thought he could read that one. The other kids would have laughed at his choice, calling it a "baby book." Reading was really hard for him; he didn't know very many words. He was pretty sure he could get through that book, though.

The dog sat expectantly beside him, panting lightly. The boy opened the book and started to read. He stumbled over a few words on the first page, but the dog kept listening attentively. The boy gave him a scratch behind the ear, turned the page, and read on. He got stuck on a word, but the man helped him with it, and he continued.

The story made him laugh; it was about a farting dog. When the boy finished the book, the dog placed his wet nose on his cheek, as if to say, "Thanks for the story." The boy smiled and gave the dog a pat. This was fun!

Dr. David Richardson is a soft-spoken veterinary surgeon in the North Sydney area of Nova Scotia. In October 2002, while listening to the radio, Dr. Richardson heard a program describing the work that Intermountain Therapy Animals in Utah has been doing. They use dogs to help children with learning disabilities become better readers. Dr. Richardson became very interested in the idea, and he contacted Kathy Klotz, executive director of ITA, to find out more about the program.

Dr. Richardson was involved for some time with the St. John Ambulance therapy dog program as an evaluator; the program had been in place in Cape Breton since 2000. The idea of taking the dogs' training a step further, and having them work with young readers, appealed to Dr. Richardson.

Dr. Richardson had three English setters of his own who were St. John Ambulance–approved therapy dogs, and who were also trained to work in the R.E.A.D. program. His wife's dog, Rainbow, was a lovely nine-year-old female. Two of her pups stayed with Dr. Richardson and his wife, and Arthur showed a great affinity for working with children. He spent time in the pediatrics ward at the hospital and he did a wonderful job in the R.E.A.D. program.

R.E.A.D. is a program that allows children who have learning difficulties or who are reluctant readers to read aloud to dogs. For many children, reading is hard work, and they find no joy in the printed word. Often their difficulties create opportunities for ridicule or embarrassment at school. R.E.A.D. tries to make the reading experience a relaxing, enjoyable time with a buddy who will never tease, correct, or evaluate them. Because dogs are

Arthur was a good listener when Jordan read to him.

non-judgmental, the children are not self-conscious about their choice of reading material or about making mistakes. Reading aloud to dogs is stress-free, and so it becomes enjoyable. The more a person practices reading, the better they become at it, just like with any other skill, and so the children in the R.E.A.D. program soon progress in their reading abilities.

The role of the dog handler is that of facilitator. The handler wants to make the reading time fun, to keep the dog alert as the children read, and to prompt the children if they get stuck on a word. Reading sessions last for about fifteen minutes.

Dr. Richardson and Arthur began working with Jordan Noble, a seven-year-old grade two student, who was enrolled at Seton Elementary in North Sydney. Dr. Richardson had known Jordan's mother for some time; she kept house for him and looked after the dogs when he and his wife went away. When Arthur received his R.E.A.D. training, Dr. Richardson approached Nancy Noble about the idea of having Jordan read to Arthur. He knew that Jordan was having difficulties with reading, and thought it would be good practice for both the boy and the dog.

Nancy Noble had become quite concerned about Jordan's frustration at school. He was losing confidence in himself, and he was making up excuses to come home early. He seemed to be falling further and further behind with his schoolwork. She knew that Jordan liked and trusted Dr. Richardson, and so she was willing to give the R.E.A.D. program a try.

Little did she know what a marvellous success it would be for Jordan. At first, he was rather fidgety and nervous as he read to the brown and white English setter, Arthur, and the weekly Sunday sessions were only about five minutes long. The books Jordan read were picture books with very little text.

Jordan really enjoyed reading to Arthur, though, and so with every session he became a bit more relaxed and confident.

Jordan said, "It's fun and great...I love reading to that dog." He felt that Arthur was really listening and that gave Jordan the incentive to keep reading.

As the sessions progressed, Jordan's focus increased, and the books got longer and more difficult. He progressed from picture books to chapter books. At the end of grade four, Jordan was reading Robert Louis Stevenson's *Treasure Island*!

Jordan declared happily, "I can read a lot in school. Any book the teacher gives me, I can read it."

Jordan's self-esteem blossomed. He no longer felt that he was "dumb" or that school was too hard. He felt that he could tackle the schoolwork with confidence. Even math was easier because he could read and understand the word problems.

Jordan developed a love for books that previously would have seemed impossible. He went to the library and took out four books at a time. He also began to read to his younger sister, sharing his love for books with her.

Since Jordan started the R.E.A.D. program with Arthur and Dr. Richardson, he moved to another school, St. Mary's, where he was enrolled in a smaller class and received extra help. These steps also helped move Jordan ahead with his reading skills. But his mother believed that reading to Arthur was a vital first step for Jordan to gain confidence and the desire to read.

Other students have benefited from the R.E.A.D. program as well. The principal of Seton Elementary, Sandra Kelly, was willing to try R.E.A.D. as a pilot project. One child with a nasogastric tube found it was a great relief to have a canine audience that didn't care if some of his words came out a bit garbled when he read. For an extremely shy child, the dog became a conduit between herself and an adult. For children who didn't have books or family members at home who enjoyed reading, it gave them that pleasant, shared reading time they had never had before.

Starting in the fall of 2004, four R.E.A.D. teams went regularly into the Wilfred Oran Library in North Sydney to read with children there. Beginning in March 2005, because of the success of the program at that library, R.E.A.D. teams also began visiting the Regional Library in Sydney. They worked with eight to twelve children each day that they were scheduled to be there.

R.E.A.D. grew in the Sydney area, with approximately fifty dogs in the program. There was no specific breed of dog that was used, but all R.E.A.D. dogs had to pass the St. John Ambulance therapy dog training, work for a year in public settings, and then pass the three-month training course for R.E.A.D.

Some dogs, like Arthur, were naturals at listening intently to the children as they read. The children read directly to them, and patted them as they read, so the dogs stayed engaged. However, if the dog seemed to be losing focus, Dr. Richardson had some simple tricks that kept the reader and dog connected for the full fifteen minutes.

Dr. Richardson taught his dogs to "place" a paw, or to point. When given the signal, the dog placed its paw on the page of the book. So, if the reading session needed a little action to keep it going, Dr. Richardson would ask a question about the story, knowing that the answer was in the picture on the page next to his dog. Then he'd give the signal for Arthur to point, and the dog placed his paw on the picture, showing the child that he'd been listening carefully to the story and knew the answer to the question. This never failed to delight the readers.

Another command Dr. Richardson taught his dogs was to "touch" with their noses. At the signal, they put their noses on his hand. If Dr. Richardson wanted Arthur to nuzzle the child sometime during the reading session, he'd place his hand near the child's head, and quietly give the touch command.

The R.E.A.D. program was completely voluntary and books were purchased through donations. In the Sydney area, they kept a selection of easy-to-read, entertaining stories that the children loved. Once a child mastered reading a book, it became his or hers to keep.

The children's smiles as they read to the dogs and their new-found pleasure in books can not be denied. Arthur and all the other R.E.A.D. dogs are making a huge impact on the lives of those young people.

GOING HOME

Some folks love life on the open road. Home is wherever they hang their hat. Others feel a great connection to a particular place and that is always home to them.

It seems that animals are the same. Some are wanderers. Others know that they are meant to be living with one special family, and they will do amazing things in order to remain there.

Mr. Blue Eyes

Kathleen Murphy and her partner Brendan Dunbar started Raven's Haven, a small non-profit cat rescue centre located in Dartmouth, Nova Scotia, in 2003.

One of their memorable rescues was an unforgettable Siamese cat. Kathleen received a phone call from Corinne Snow in the Woodlawn area of Dartmouth in July 2004. A purebred, sealpoint Siamese cat had arrived in her backyard, looking for food. He'd been prowling around the neighbourhood for a while, getting handouts here and there. Corinne had managed to pick him up to cuddle him and had discovered that he had a nasty cut on his leg. She'd called a vet who suggested that she contact Raven's Haven.

Brendan and Kathleen drove from Raven's Haven out to Woodlawn to pick up the cat. They thought it was unusual for a purebred Siamese to become a stray, but when they saw his condition, there was no doubt that he had been on his own for some time.

Kathleen and Brendan took the Siamese cat to the vet. He was malnourished and had a fever. He had blood work done and was put on antibiotics. It was arranged that he would return to the vet in two weeks, when he was stronger, for his vaccines and neutering.

Corinne offered to foster the cat, who she called Mr. Blue Eyes. She already felt a strong bond with him, and her five-year-old daughter liked him, too.

Perhaps he would have simply settled happily into Corinne's family except that Corinne's boyfriend had an allergy to cats. As well, Corinne ran a daycare from her home and the cat wasn't too crazy about all the children's noise and activity.

So, at the end of the two weeks, Raven's Haven said a home had been located for the Siamese. When Kathleen and

Tai (Mr. Blue Eyes) and his friend, Tieryn.

Brendan arrived at Corinne's to take Mr. Blue Eyes, there was a very emotional farewell. Corinne did not really want to give up this cat. Mr. Blue Eyes lashed his tail and narrowed his eyes. He also seemed very angry and depressed when he realized that he was being separated from Corinne.

Corinne donated a blanket and other personal items for Mr. Blue Eyes to take to his new home and, teary-eyed, she left him with Kathleen.

Corinne was resigned to let Mr. Blue Eyes go, but the cat had other ideas. He found a way to freedom by clawing a hole in the bathroom window screen and he escaped.

When Kathleen learned that Mr. Blue Eyes was again on his own, she phoned Corinne to tell her the news. She said that, however unlikely, the Siamese might turn up at her place.

The cat would have to travel a good five kilometres through busy downtown city streets to reach her, but Kathleen remembered the cat's feisty, determined look. She wanted Corinne to keep an eye out for him, just in case.

About a month later, Corinne was caring for her daycare charges when one child looked out the window and yelled, "A cat's out there!"

Corinne didn't dare hope that it was Mr. Blue Eyes. She rushed to the window, and sitting in her back yard, just as he had two months before, was the Siamese.

Corinne was overjoyed. She almost couldn't believe that Mr. Blue Eyes had found his way back to her. But here he was! Their reunion was magical, full of love and a sense of destiny.

Corinne checked him over to make sure he was all right. He seemed to be fine. In fact, it was obvious that sometime during his travels another family had taken him in and had planned to keep him, because now he was neutered! His heart belonged to Corinne, though, and somehow he had found his way back to her.

Corinne called Kathleen at Raven's Haven to give her the news. There was no question now of whether or not he would stay. Corinne's sister, Leanne, resided in the other half of the duplex where Corinne lived and she agreed to keep Mr. Blue Eyes. That way, he would be close to Corinne but the daycare and allergy problems would be circumvented.

Leanne named the cat Tai. He lived in the lap of luxury, with top-of-the-line food, silky blankets, and two families who loved him.

Despite his dislike for the daycare hubbub, Tai proved to have a have important mission in life with Leanne's little girl, Tieryn. Tieryn was autistic.

Autism is a disorder in which children find the stimuli of the world confusing. For autistic children, communication and social interaction are very difficult.

Leanne was concerned about Tieryn because other children found it hard to play with her, not realizing how difficult oral language was for her. Voices often sounded more like the teacher's garbled "wah, wah, wah" in Charlie Brown cartoons than sensible messages. Leanne feared that Tieryn would be lonesome and would not be able to develop her social skills.

Tai became Tieryn's best friend. Tai spoke with body language, and she soon learned that his purr meant he was happy, and a scratch meant he was angry. It was very clear.

Through playing with Tai, and hearing her family talk about what they were doing together, Tieryn learned to say words like "run," "tired," "Tai," "eating," and "sleeping." This was a major breakthrough for the little girl.

Tieryn could be who she really was with Tai and not feel frustrated. Leanne thought of him as a miracle cat because of how much he drew Tieryn out of her shell.

Mr. Blue Eyes (Tai) had travelled many city kilometres and had escaped from at least two other well-meaning homes in order to be in this place. This was where he knew he needed to be.

Puff may have been born in a barn but he looked like an aristocrat.

Puff

Elizabeth Archer has always had a great affection for animals. Living in the city makes it difficult for her to have pets around her like she had when she was a youngster. She cherishes her memories, though, and has passed her love of animals on to her own daughters.

Growing up in Ontario, Elizabeth was a real horse nut. Her horse was boarded at a neighborhood stable, and as you may imagine, Elizabeth spent a good deal of her time there. One day she found kittens crawling around the hay pile in the horse barn. One was especially pretty; he had long, cream-coloured fur. Elizabeth asked her mother, Colleen, if they could please take him home.

Well, he was awfully cute. Even though his mother was a barn cat, his father was a Persian. He looked like a tiny aristocrat.

Being born and raised in a barn, though, meant he was feral. He'd never been handled, and as far as he was concerned, he was quite happy to keep it that way. But once Elizabeth and Colleen decided that they wanted him, the stable owner, Nanette, felt it was in his best interest to end his barn-roving days. She spent a long time clamouring around the hayloft, chasing this kitten down. Finally, she nabbed him and brought him to the cat carrier.

Unfortunately, the kitten saw the carrier as a trap and made a panicked launch through the door before Colleen could get it closed and latched, and the kitten hunt was on again.

Eventually, the cream-colored kitten, Puff, did come to live with Colleen, Elizabeth, and the rest of their family, and although it took some time for him to learn to trust humans and to settle into domesticity, he did become very affectionate. He even learned to do some simple tricks, like begging for cheese.

Puff developed a wonderful and unusual relationship with the family's collie, Mackie. At first, neither dog nor kitten was impressed with the presence of the other. Gradually they got used to one another, and after a month or so, they became the best of friends.

Mackie allowed Puff to share his dinner, and they slept curled up together. Puff would sometimes play with the long hairs on Mackie's tail, which the old collie affectionately tolerated. Puff also liked to hold the old dog's face between his paws to kiss his whitening muzzle.

One time a neighbour's dog came into their yard. Elizabeth saw the dog chase Puff around the corner of Mackie's pen. The next thing Elizabeth saw was the neighbour's dog making a beeline for home, with Mackie close on his heels. Mackie made sure no one else was going to chase *his* cat.

When Mackie's health declined and he had to be euthanized, Puff was devastated. He spent the first night of his friend's absence out in the freezing rain searching for the old dog.

Puff could not seem to reconcile himself to Mackie's passing. He became depressed and sick. The family soon decided to adopt a Shetland sheepdog pup, Vicky, and they hoped Puff would be drawn out of his grief by this energetic new dog.

The pup and the cat did become friends, and although their relationship was very different from Puff's and Mackie's, it was special in its own way.

Puff's relationships with the dogs in the family were quite remarkable, but his communication with people at a crucial time was even more amazing.

Vicky and Puff were separated when Colleen's family moved from Peterborough to Deep River. The family was moving temporarily into a small rental house. Puff was used to prowling his neighbourhood, and they didn't think he'd be too happy in the new living quarters.

The people who bought their place in Peterborough seemed to like the handsome cream-coloured cat and expressed an interest in keeping him. It saddened Colleen's family to leave him behind, but they thought Puff would be much happier staying where he'd be able to visit his old haunts, and so when moving day came, Puff stayed behind.

Three months later, Colleen and her family were ready to move into their present home, a nice country place with a horse barn and many kilometres of riding trails. The day before they were scheduled to move, Colleen's best friend, Sue, phoned her from Peterborough.

"Do you want your cat back?" Sue asked.

The family that had bought the Peterborough house apparently hadn't gotten along well with Puff. They weren't letting him into the house, and he wasn't being fed properly.

Puff had turned up at Sue's door that morning, meowing and crying until she finally let him in. Puff hadn't been to Sue's house in the three months since Colleen had moved away. But there he was, insistent that she let him in. She recognized him as Colleen's cat, and called the new owners of the house. They made it plain that they did not want Puff.

Of course Colleen wanted him back!

Sue put Puff in a cat carrier. (No doubt Sue found it easier to get him into it than the first time it was attempted, up in the hayloft of Nanette's barn!) She drove him to Deep River to join his family on the day that they moved into their new home.

Somehow Puff knew that Sue was the one person in Peterborough he could count on to help him. He knew that his real family could take him again, even after three months of separation, and that they were moving into a farm where he would be happy. Only Puff knows for sure how he knew all this, but he certainly ended up where he wanted to be, at the precise time when it could all work out.

Tim is a black-over-tan German shepherd.

POLICE SERVICE DOG TIM

Tim is a colossal black-over-tan German shepherd who was imported by the RCMP from a broker in the Czech Republic. When he was nine months old, Police Service Dog Tim, regiment number 575, was tested by Innisfail RCMP police dog staff as a potential police dog. Having passed all the required tests, Tim was then shipped to his handler and partner, Corporal Rick Bushey. Rick, originally from Miramichi, New Brunswick, was stationed at New Minas, Nova Scotia, at the time.

When Tim was about one-and-a-half-years-old, he and Rick attended Innisfail, Alberta, the national training center for RCMP dogs. They underwent four gruelling months of training. Tim and Rick satisfactorily completed all requirements specified in the course and they graduated in December.

Every year following that, Tim had validation in all aspects of his work, from explosives to fieldwork. Rick was required to complete a physical examination every year as well. It was important for him to be able to keep up with his partner, whether they were searching for a missing person or chasing down a suspect.

RCMP service dog training is rigorous, and the dogs must learn to obey commands willingly and immediately. Tim did this, but he also proved to be a very intelligent, dedicated police dog. Some of the successes that Rick and Tim enjoyed in their work were because of Tim's persistence, his ability to think, and Rick's trust in his teammate.

On May 19, 2001, Rick and Tim were called to assist when two subjects escaped from the Kings Correctional Centre in Waterville, Kings County, Nova Scotia. It was believed that the suspects were fleeing on foot.

Tim picked up the trail at the correctional centre and began the hunt.

The snow was off the ground by this time, but it was a cool spring day and the ground underfoot was wet. The track led them through all sorts of terrain, and most of it was hard going. They travelled along gravel roads, on old ATV tracks, into ploughed fields and orchards, through bush and town residential areas. At one point, they had to track the subjects through swampland where the water came up to Rick's shoulders. Tim swam through the bitterly cold, brackish water and continued on the scent. Rick followed Tim unquestioningly through this punishing cross-country trail, having complete confidence in his dog's abilities.

The suspects were eventually reported near the peat moss plant near Berwick. Although Tim was so tired that he vomited twice along the trail, he did not slacken in his pursuit. At last, Rick and Tim could hear the two suspects ahead of them. Tim increased his pace. Rick and Tim came into a clearing in the bush and sighted the two men. The suspects turned, and seeing the dog and Rick close behind them, they gave up their flight, falling to the ground. Tim ran forward and lay on top of the suspects, holding them until officers could take charge of the situation.

Tim had tracked the two escapees over sixteen kilometres, through dense bush, into bone-chilling water that was as black as tar, and over rough ground. He did not for a moment give less than his best, and in the end, it meant the successful completion of his task.

Another example of Tim's determination to get the job done occurred when, one fall night, there was a report of gunshots being fired in the Berwick area. When the police investigated, they found suspects in a vehicle out in a field, but they couldn't find a weapon. It's pretty hard to charge someone for discharging a firearm if there doesn't appear to be any gun around.

The area was scoured with no success. Tim and Rick were called in to search. Twice Tim went off on his own to a clump of bushes. At first, Rick thought he was losing his focus and was just nosing around. Then he decided to check on what Tim was finding so interesting.

What Rick discovered under those bushes was a revolver. At that point, charges could be laid.

Tim's desire to see his task completed helped to save a woman's life. In April 2004, a middle-aged lady went missing from her King's County home. She had been intoxicated, was on medication, and was possibly suicidal, so there was great concern for her safety.

Tim and Rick began their search in the evening. The ground was wet; the night was clear and cool.

Tim located her track on an old ski trail and followed it for about three kilometres. At last, they came to an abandoned barn out in the middle of nowhere. It looked like it hadn't been used in years.

Tim entered the barn and Rick followed. Rick shone his flashlight around the interior of the building, but saw nothing to suggest that the woman had been there. He turned and walked out, calling Tim after him.

Tim circled back and re-entered the barn. Rick felt sure that he'd checked inside carefully, and he wondered what Tim was up to. He called him back outside. A third time Tim went into the barn. This time, he started to paw at some old hay that was piled in one corner.

Rick stepped over to see what Tim had found. He shone his light into the corner. Under the hay, the woman lay sleeping. When the night air had turned chill she'd blanketed herself with the hay.

Tim was alert and ready to respond to his partner's command.

Fortunately, the woman was all right and she was returned to her home. Had Tim not been so persistent in making Rick understand that she was in the barn, it might have been a long time before she was found.

Tim saved many people in his years with the force. In the Windsor area, he was called to locate a fifteen-year-old girl who had disappeared from her home one winter day. She was in her bare feet and clad only in her pyjamas. Finding her before hypothermia set in was crucial.

The girl had left her home around ten o'clock in the morning. As one would expect, her family and neighbours were very concerned and by mid-afternoon many of them had been out looking for her. When Tim and Rick arrived at the house, they found that the track was muddled up with the scents of many people. This would not be an easy track.

Tim did eventually find the girl, curled up under a tree, wrapped in a small blanket. Rick took off his socks and put them on the girl's feet, securing them on her legs with his gaiters. He kept his boots on in case he needed to carry the girl to safety.

Tim walked ahead of Rick and the girl, showing them the easiest route back out of the woods. It wasn't long before they returned to the girl's driveway. She was examined and taken to hospital by EHS.

Tim showed time and again that he could read Rick's intent and the situation and know if there was danger involved. Tim was trained in aggression, and he could certainly be aggressive if that was what was called for, but he could also show concern if a victim had need of him. Rick had no worries that Tim would bite an innocent person.

An old gentleman, in his eighties, became lost in the woods while hunting. Rick and Tim were brought in to aid in the search. Tim picked up the elderly man's scent and ran ahead of Rick. When Rick caught up to him, Tim was sitting next to the elderly gentleman, being patted affectionately on the head. Tim even searched for and located the elderly man's hunting firearm, which he'd dropped in his confusion. The gentleman felt that Tim was a very special dog.

In February 2003, there was an armed robbery in Kentville, Nova Scotia. The suspect took off in a vehicle. The abandoned vehicle was later located in the nearby community of Centreville by RCMP members. The suspect had fled on foot.

Rick and Tim were brought to the scene and they checked the vehicle. Tim began to track the suspect through a snowy field. Darkness had fallen and the cold was bone chilling. The police were very conscious that somewhere, out in the darkness, there was an armed suspect. Tim and the officers waded through the snow, alert and cautious.

Tim climbed over a snowbank and down into a foxhole. Rick had the dog on a long leash at that time. Because of the snow, the hole, and the thickness of the surrounding bushes, Rick couldn't see Tim. He thought Tim must have squeezed into the foxhole after the suspect and landed on top of him. He realized he was quite right when, after a moment, the suspect yelled, "Get the dog off me or I'll shoot him!"

Rick called Tim off and they moved some distance away.

Many more officers arrived and a two-hour negotiation began between the police and the suspect. Eventually the suspect stood up and set his rifle close at hand, leaning it against a tree. He bargained with the police for cigarettes and water, but the officers couldn't get him to come out of the bushes, to give up the gun, or to calm down. He was strung out on drugs, and kept threatening to kill them and himself.

At last, the suspect moved about a metre away from his rifle. Rick felt this was the best chance they'd get. He gave Tim the command to take him.

Despite the distractions of bitter cold, lights and sirens, police officers coming and going, and the long negotiations, Tim

Tim saved many lives during his career.

was ready, alert, and focused. When Rick gave the command, Tim sprang at the suspect and knocked him down. The officers were then able to seize the loaded rifle and take the suspect into custody.

Tim was credited with saving the lives of the police officers at the scene. He knew his job, knew what had to be done, and he did it without hesitation.

Tim was rewarded for this act of bravery by being inducted into the Purina Animal Hall of Fame in April 2005.

Rick and his daughter wrote a poem to commemorate Tim's Hall of Fame Award.

Tim

Man's best friend
What does it mean
I don't know what it is to
    you
But it is this to me

It's endless devotion
    through thick and thin
It's long walks and talks,
    that leave me with a
    grin

It's the courage and
    confidence he passes
    on to me,
It's on those dark and
    dreary nights that with
    his eyes I see.

It's in the tug of the leash
    when my energy seems
    done
It's in knowing that with
    pull and tug he
    continues to run.

It's in knowing that
    whatever I face he is
    always by my side

It's the fact that he
    always listens ready to
    abide

It's in having a friend and a
    partner that I need so
    much
It's the feeling that as time
    goes on it only gets
    stronger as such.

It's this bond that grows
    stronger with each
    passing day,
That makes my partner my
    best friend in every
    possible way.

It's in the hope as years
    pass by and his energy
    starts to dim
That I'll be there to return
    the love and devotion
    that has been given to
    me by Tim.

PSD Tim was an invaluable asset to the force. The work that he performed caused criminals to be apprehended and lives to be saved. He and Rick Bushey were a team, learning from one another, and enjoying the work they did together.

ANIMAL COMMUNICATORS

Animal communicators are people with the ability to receive information from animals and to send messages to them telepathically. They are aware of images, words, and emotions that animals transmit.

Animal communication is not a common career choice. School guidance councillors don't recommend it as an option. Community colleges don't offer it as a course. So how does one become an animal communicator?

It appears to be a calling. An animal communicator usually receives gentle nudges from animals to follow along that path. Then one finds a mentor who guides and encourages the skills that have already come to light.

The road to becoming an animal communicator tends to be full of interesting twists and turns, but the awareness one develops is deep and fulfilling.

In this section, you will meet three animal communicators who have learned to listen to the gentle voices of animals.

Maggie Carruthers

Maggie has been a therapeutic touch practitioner for several years. She realized that when she worked on animals, she often received images and emotions from them.

Thinking back, though, she felt that her cat, Flous, really sent her along the path to becoming an animal communicator, giving her messages that she couldn't ignore. She'd had Flous for fourteen years, and although she'd loved her dearly, she hadn't thought that there was anything particularly unusual about her. Her only distinguishing qualities were that her fur never seemed to get wet, she liked to play like a dog, and she had very dexterous paws that could hold objects, such as pencils.

When Flous was thirteen, she developed a growth on her jaw. It wasn't cancerous, but it gradually ate away at the jawbone. Because of Flous' age, it was too dangerous to try reconstructive surgery. Maggie and the vet treated the cat as best they could.

Maggie asked Flous to please let her know when it got to be too much for her; that when it was time for her to "pass on," Maggie would help ease her pain with euthanasia, if that was what Flous wanted.

Ten months later, Maggie began to dream about another cat in various stages of life, from a tiny, helpless kitten, just opening her eyes, to a mature cat in the prime of her life. It took Maggie a while to realize that she was getting a message from a cat that would be coming to live with her sometime in the future.

Almost a year to the day after Maggie had asked Flous to tell her when she was ready to slip from this life, she knew it was time to ask the vet to make a house call, and Flous was euthanized.

It was very difficult for Maggie to deal with the loss of her companion. She missed her terribly. Her days were empty. Even simple errands like shopping for groceries became ordeals because she would have to pass the pet food aisle.

One day, she had to pick up office supplies for work, and she noticed a book about cats on a discount table. It was a book that had pictures and blurbs about various breeds. Maggie picked the book up and thumbed through it.

She came to a picture that reminded her so much of Flous, it made her heart ache. The cat's colouring wasn't exactly the same, but there were striking similarities. Maggie read the write-up about the breed. The pictured cat was a Norwegian Forest cat. They were known to have fur that repelled water. Other distinguishing characteristics were just like Flous.

Maggie was quite sure that Flous hadn't been a purebred, but now there was no doubt in her mind that she'd had Norwegian Forest cat in her blood. She started to research the breed. It is rare in Canada, but Maggie found a breeder in Quebec through the Internet.

Maggie continued to dream about a dark cat with a pink nose, white chest and white paws. She came to believe that this cat in her dreams was to be her next feline companion.

Maggie went to Montreal on an annual basis, and one of those trips was coming up. She was so sure that she would find the cat of her dreams on that trip that she packed a cat carrier in the car.

When she got to Montreal, she phoned the breeder of Norwegian Forest cats. The breeder said that they had no cats for sale. Their cat wouldn't have kittens for weeks, and when they were born, they were all spoken for. But they knew another breeder who lived in Kingston, Ontario. Would Maggie like her phone number?

Maggie called the other breeder. That breeder had a kitten that perfectly fit the description of the cat from Maggie's dreams. But the breeder said she planned to leave for southern Ontario that very day to take the kitten to her grandson. Maggie asked if she could please come to see the kitten. The breeder agreed, so Maggie drove three hours to Kingston. The moment she saw the kitten, she knew she had to have her. It was exactly the cat she had dreamt of for the last six months.

Maggie's the kind of person who believes in adopting animals from shelters, but this cat had been calling to her for months. She bought the cat, content that she had her Flous back, reincarnated as this youngster.

Maggie started back to Nova Scotia during a dreadful snowstorm. She stopped along the way at a friend's house and slept on the kitchen floor for the night. Her new cat, named Uffie, stayed with her. She noted on that very first night how Uffie played with her toys in exactly the same way that Flous had done.

Maggie had to make another stop for the night in Fredericton, New Brunswick. The storm made travelling slow going. She was pleased and impressed with how calm and trusting the kitten was during the long drive home. She didn't cry at all.

A Norwegian Forest cat

Her experiences with Flous during her last year of life and Uffie's communication through Maggie's dreams prodded Maggie onto the road to being an animal communicator.

Maggie soon began to dream of a cat again. This time, the cat had a coat that looked like the flesh pattern on a mackerel fish, with a little bit of white on his neck and on one back paw. She contacted Uffie's breeder and found that she had just such a cat. In fact, it was a half-brother to Uffie. Of course, this cat found his home with Maggie as well.

She named the second cat Skogheegan, because in Scandinavia this breed is known as Skog cats, Norse folklore cats. Maggie feels Skogheegan has taught her how to be a true communicator.

In 2004, a new cat came into Maggie's life. It was her mum's fluffy gray and white cat, Angel. If it hadn't been for Angel, Maggie's mother may have died when she fell and broke her hip in her house in St. Lambert.

Maggie hadn't heard from her mother on her birthday, which was unusual. When she couldn't reach her the next day, which was Mother's Day, Maggie became very concerned. By that Monday, when she still couldn't reach her mum, Maggie felt desperate to find a way to contact her. She knew that her mum was an active church member, so Maggie phoned the church's caretaker. He lived just two doors down from Maggie's mother, and was a good friend of hers. He agreed to check on her.

> Every time Maggie Carruthers makes contact with an animal, it is a profound experience for her. She learns about the animal, but also, she learns more about herself.

He tried calling her first, and when she didn't answer the phone, he went to the house and knocked on the door. Still, he got no reply. He went around to the back and peered in through the patio doors. The screening obscured his view of the interior of the house, and so he didn't see Maggie's mother lying on the floor. However, after a moment, he glimpsed Angel's light fur. The cat was sitting next to Maggie's mother, and the white fur she had shed made an outline of the fallen woman's body on the floor. The caretaker was able to make out the woman's silhouette in the white hair and realized that she was in distress. Had the cat not kept a vigil beside Maggie's mum, and had not shed her bright white fur all around her, the caretaker would not have noticed her and would have assumed that she was not at home.

Regrettably, Maggie's mum passed away soon after this. In the time between her fall and her death, Angel became close to Maggie and now makes her home with her new human friend.

Maggie sees herself as a facilitator and an interpreter. She likes to get to know the animals that she works with. She usually does therapeutic touch as part of her communication; she feels that the touch helps to activate the animal's memories. She senses the animal's emotions and perceives images of what he or she has seen.

Owners often call Maggie to their homes to help them with troubled pets. She takes as much time as she needs in order to allow each animal to share his or her energy, process it, and then let go of what needs to be released, move on, and allow the animal to heal. This may take weeks. She gives suggestions to owners about ways they can make the environment a more pleasant place for the animal and for improving their own communication skills with their animal companion. She often sees herself as a mediator between the animal and its owner.

Every time Maggie Carruthers makes contact with an animal, it is a profound experience for her. She learns about the animal, but also, she learns more about herself. She knows that animals are here to elevate us energetically and spiritually. They have a far greater awareness of themselves, of life, and of death than we do. They are not just fixtures in the home.

Maggie marvels at how animals understand how to be healers just by being present. They know how to perform therapy without the use of words. They know that the energies of play and companionship are vital components of life.

She feels that we can learn so much by observing animals and seeing how they cope with stress. The amount of abuse many animals deal with is staggering, and yet they tend to remain loving, giving, and trusting. Animals' patience with us is phenomenal.

Maggie believes that being an animal communicator is a great privilege and not one to be taken lightly. Although anyone can learn to listen and hear what animals are trying to communicate to us, there is an ethical, moral, and spiritual responsibility to help them be better understood. She says, "Messages are there if we just quiet ourselves and listen."

She once had an interview on CBC radio, and she took along her dog, Bear. Bear, being a Labrador retriever, was a big, puppy-like bundle of energy.

Maggie asked him, on the air, what he wanted to tell people. What he relayed, through Maggie, was this: "Animals want to be treated equally. They are equal to humans."

Maggie is devoting her life to get that message across to as many people as she can.

Calloway M'Cloud

The journey that brought Calloway M'Cloud to Unicorn Farm near Montague, Prince Edward Island, was filled with difficulties and soul-searching. Calloway was happy with where the path led her and felt that the work she was doing was honest and fulfilling.

This trek began when Calloway was a very young girl, growing up in Pennsylvania. As a six-year-old, she intuitively understood that animals had a special means of communication that did not involve vocalization. She was fascinated by the idea, but her academic parents gave her little encouragement. At best, they humoured her notion as a child's flight of fancy.

Calloway, a precocious youngster, set out to prove to herself that animals could communicate in a sophisticated, telepathic way. She felt that once she had this proof, she would become Translator for All the Animals.

Calloway thought about this very seriously. She felt that since snails are simple creatures, their communications would be simple. She became determined to communicate with the snails that lived in a nearby stream. She spent hours next to an old gristmill, peering into the water and concentrating on the snails, willing them to move in a way that she directed. She was totally crestfallen when, despite her dedication and desire, she did not seem to get through to a single snail.

Then she thought that if she made her smell more notice-able, animals would find it easier to approach her. Calloway went through a period of not using soap, hoping to enhance her smell for the wildlife that lived around their home. The animals didn't seem to notice her any more than before, and the people in her life didn't appreciate her new experiment. Eventually, she chalked it up as another failure.

She tried to communicate with the family dog telepathically. She gave the dog a voice command, "sit," and the dog obeyed willingly. Then she tried to think the command. The dog didn't respond.

She despaired that she wasn't getting any encouragement from animals at all about telepathic communication. "I needed a bird to come perch on my head... Here I was, this good-inten-tioned person and they were all ignoring me." Around the age of ten, Calloway was completely discouraged and let the idea go.

Then she decided if she couldn't communicate with animals in one way, she'd help them in another. She'd become a veteri-narian. She threw herself into this new passion, getting a job as a vet's assistant and looking into application forms for veterinary colleges at the age of eleven.

A stumbling block to this plan was that she became dizzy and faint when she helped the vet during procedures that caused the animal pain or produced blood. People told her that she would eventually overcome that problem, and so she continued with her plan.

Gradually, she did have less trouble with fainting. One day, she had to help the vet with a large orange cat that needed to have a painful procedure. At first, she felt the familiar buzzing in her head, but she got through the incident without fainting.

At first, she felt proud of herself for getting beyond her dizziness. Then she realized that the reason she was able to do so was because she had shifted her thoughts and feelings about the cat. In her mind it was no longer a living, breathing creature, but only a lump of fur and flesh and bones on the examining room table. She had distanced herself from the animal, making it an object. She did not like the feeling at all. She felt like she was becoming an animal mechanic. She chose not to become a vet.

This left her wondering what she should do. She didn't have a passion to commit to any longer, and she was at an age when others expected her to make the decision about what to do when she grew up. Her father was a professor of English, and so she thought she would follow in his footsteps.

Calloway was a capable student and she did very well with her studies. As she was doing her graduate school courses in Virginia, however, she realized that it wasn't making a lot of sense to her. The world of academia wasn't the real world. There seemed to be a lot of politics and posturing. She was trying to fit in, but that life did not fit her.

She was making straight A's even though she was not trying to excel. Shortly before she was to graduate, she realized that she couldn't bear to continue on this path.

Calloway was at a loss. She felt she'd tried and failed for the third time in her young life. She developed a severe eating disorder. It was a dark time for her.

About this time, her maternal grandmother called her from Indiana. A friend of hers had rescued a litter of puppies and she felt that Calloway needed to have one of them. She announced over the phone, "I have a dog for you." With that summons, Calloway drove for nine hours to Indiana to pick up a young Labrador-retriever cross that she named Books. Little did the grandmother realize that her phone call would save her granddaughter's and a puppy's life.

> " Because of seven years of meditations and listening to her inner voice, her "boiled potato language," to help her with the eating disorder, she seemed to be a natural when it came to opening herself to animal communication.

Calloway became despondent over her seemingly meaningless life, and she seriously contemplated suicide. What held her from the brink of that fatal decision was her dog. Nothing else really mattered, but she didn't know what would happen to Books if she were to kill herself. In order to care for her puppy, she chose to live.

Her life took a profound turning, and she credits many of the changes to Books.

Calloway realized that since she'd made the decision to live and take care of Books, she needed to take better care of herself. Her eating disorder would have to be brought under control.

Calloway meditated, trying to determine the right food choice for her, and the image that came to her was a plain, boiled potato. She knew she could eat a potato.

"It was perfect. It didn't feel threatening. It just felt very, very safe and simple. That's what I needed."

That was the beginning of her healing. She started to eat again, picking nutritious foods that she knew would be right for her. Her diet was limited, but wholesome. Her health improved.

Calloway used her inner voice to guide her to make other decisions. She was estranged from her family and had to rely upon herself to navigate through the world.

Calloway heard of an animal communicator, Patty Summers, in Virginia. She was interested in her work, but after her feelings of failure when trying to communicate with animals as a child, she wasn't prepared at that time to meet her. However, after moving to a new home, her cat started the very unpleasant habit of peeing on her pillow. Calloway tried to solve this problem on her own, with no success, and finally consulted Patty Summers about it.

During their session, Patty explained that the cat was not happy with the move and was acting out of frustration. Calloway then had a talk with her cat, and the problem was resolved.

Even then, Calloway wasn't motivated to take a class from Patty Summers until a horse-trainer friend of hers mentioned that her daughter really wanted to attend one of Patty's animal communication workshops, but she didn't want to go alone. Calloway was persuaded to accompany the daughter. Calloway said she, "ended up there, but not for me." She opened up to what was being presented and joined in the exercises.

She found the session overpowering. Because of seven years of meditations and listening to her inner voice, her " boiled potato language," to help her with the eating disorder, she seemed to be a natural when it came to opening herself to animal communication. "It was exhilarating to finally have got something that felt important that I was really good at."

Patty Summers started to refer clients to Calloway, and she became recognized as a professional animal communicator.

Books, a model dog most of the time, sometimes helped Calloway realize when it was time to make difficult choices. Calloway felt he was acting out stresses that she wasn't acknowledging within herself. One time, he started killing the chickens on the farm where Calloway was working and boarding. It got to the point where she would either have to get rid of Books or move. She moved. The move brought her to the place where she met the man who would become her husband.

More recently, they were living in a lovely area in the mountains, surrounded by wilderness. Calloway thought they were there to stay. Then Books began to chase and kill the neighbour's cats. Calloway begged Books not to do this, but the chasing continued and the neighbour became so irate he threatened to shoot the dog.

Calloway took Books for a long walk and she thought about what was happening. She realized that she wasn't really happy where she was living. There were stresses that she'd been blocking from her mind. She decided that Books was again telling her that it was time to move on.

She searched carefully for the perfect place to settle. Eventually, she bought Unicorn Farm, outside Montague, PEI, in 2003. She has continued with her animal communications. She also assembled a small herd of horses, mostly rescued from slaughterhouses, and began a new venture.

The people who attended Calloway's horse clinics and camps didn't learn how to horseback ride. They learned lessons about empowerment and trust from the horses.

To understand how Calloway came to this venture, we need to again visit her past. Calloway's early experiences with horse training were not positive. As a girl, she was horse crazy, and she began riding lessons when she was eleven. Her riding instructor was fairly typical of the day; she was aggressive both with the horses and with the students. Lessons were often punctuated with screams, swearing, and kicks in the horses' sides. This horrified Calloway, but being only eleven, and wanting to ride so desperately, she continued the lessons.

Calloway eventually started to give riding lessons herself. She wanted the lessons to be as gentle and meaningful for the children and the ponies as possible so she started the children off by making them ride bareback. Calloway hoped this would help build a relationship between the ponies and the children.

Still, the ponies tried to evade her when she walked up to them in their pasture. If they enjoyed what they were doing, wouldn't they come to her? Calloway decided to try something else. She called it "Horscery."

She made up activities for the children to do with the ponies that would build trust and co-operation. Calloway went on faith that what she was doing was right. The children had to meet the ponies in the pasture without ropes, halters, or whips and have

Many of Calloway's early horse experiences involved black mares.

the ponies become engaged and complete a task with them. Over time, they tried natural horsemanship, clicker training, and obstacle courses.

Calloway noted that if the children did not enter the pasture with an air of power and co-operation, they would get nowhere with the ponies. The key to success was the children's self-confidence. Calloway realized that the horses wanted the young humans to take a leadership role, and they acted in whatever way necessary to bring that out in the children. The horses were actually teaching the children to become problem-solvers and leaders.

Horscery evolved as Calloway observed people and horses working together. Horscery was not about teaching horses. It was about horses helping people to grow and trust, and to learn how to change their behaviours so they could have strong, honest relationships.

When Calloway started her five-day children's camps on PEI, she wondered if she'd bitten off more than she could chew. Many of the teenagers had a lot of resistance to what she was asking them to do, and she was aware that if they didn't see results quickly, they would lose interest completely.

At her very first camp, she remembers a girl who had been signed up for the camp by her parents because they thought it would be good for her. She had very little interest in being there, and she was very guarded.

Calloway asked the young people to go out into the field and select a horse. This girl was going to work with one of the mustangs. As Calloway observed, she became more and more concerned. The mustang would not engage with the girl at all. Calloway tried to coach the girl to help her get started. Nothing happened. Calloway felt that if she didn't intervene, the girl would throw up her hands and refuse to try anything else.

Calloway stepped in—something she rarely did—but this time it seemed to be necessary. She attempted to get the mustang's attention. The horse completely ignored her. Calloway got no feedback from the mustang at all. It was as if there was a gray fog all around her. In fact, Calloway started to worry that the horse might be ill.

Calloway grounded herself and tried once more to connect with the mustang. Suddenly, it dawned on her. The horse was acting like a sullen teenager. Calloway began to laugh. She turned to the girl and announced that the horse was mirroring her.

The girl stared at the horse for a moment, then started to laugh, too. She saw that Calloway was right. The horse was acting exactly like she was!

Realizing that the horse could pick up on her mood and throw it back at her was the incentive the girl needed to get her to try to connect with the mustang. It didn't take long before she was making personal progress and blossoming.

The young campers also did exercises away from the horses that helped them learn how to be strong and co-operative. Calloway played games with the campers and gave them responsibilities that let them develop trust and strength. Calloway hoped that "they'll get a sense of what real power—honesty—is."

Adult camps and workshops had fewer games, but the focus was still on personal growth. Often Calloway began the session by asking everyone to reflect upon a relationship they wanted clarity on. Then they went out into the field to pick a horse. They noticed which horses were drawn to them and which ones did not connect with them. Later, they discussed what the horses were communicating to them.

Participants were asked to work with the horse from the inside out. Calloway said, "The goal is to get the horse to trust and want to be with them." By doing this, the people grew and learned how to solve problems in their personal relationships.

Calloway believes that horses are such wonderful teachers because they are very spirited creatures, and yet they are balanced. They have great strength, and yet they can be gentle.

Horses have deep wisdom, and can sense what is at a person's core. People must be balanced to work with a horse successfully, and to do that they must recognize their own strengths and learn to work from a place of self-confidence or power.

Calloway loved what she was doing with Horscery, but in the future she would like to work with those who have great need to find balance in their lives. She'd like to have workshops for battered women, teens at risk, recovering addicts, and women suffering from eating disorders. She feels that with the horses' help, suffering people can be made to feel in balance again. They can learn to trust and to feel integrity.

She feels that this can happen, in time. As with everything else in her life, she has learned to trust the animals and her own wisdom.

Karen Runge

Karen Runge, a tall woman with salt-and-pepper hair, has always had an affinity for animals. As a child, even aloof animals would take to her right away. As with Calloway, her gift for connecting with animals was not encouraged, and so Karen learned to doubt her abilities. It has taken a lifetime of experiences, some animal communication courses, and wonderful mentors to help Karen trust in herself and the messages she receives.

Karen believes she took her first real steps toward becoming an animal communicator when she was living in California in the 1980s. Like Maggie Carruthers, it was a cat who nudged her onto the beginning of her journey. Karen was out for a walk one evening, feeling rather despondent over the break-up of a relationship, when she found a tiny gray and white kitten lapping water out of the gutter. Karen's heart went out to this poor unfortunate little stray and she took her home.

The kitten, who she named Sheba, was unhealthy. Karen took her to a vet. The vet felt she was beautiful, certainly worth saving, and put her on a course of antibiotics. Sheba responded well to the treatment and soon recovered.

Shortly after Sheba came to live with her, Karen was wrestling with the dilemma of whether or not to go to Switzerland to live. She made trips to Europe to check out the possibilities there. Each time she left, she put Sheba in the care of a friend.

The friend, who seemed to have a great understanding of animals, suggested to Karen that she should let the cat know how long she'd be gone each time she went away on a trip; it would decrease any anxiety Sheba might have. Karen had no idea how she'd go about telling a cat she'd be gone for a week. The friend told her to picture in her mind the sun rising and setting the appropriate number of times. Karen felt a bit foolish, but she followed her friend's advice. Upon her return from each trip, Sheba did seem to expect her home.

However, a neighbour had been taking Sheba in while Karen was away, and Sheba got so that she was staying at her place, day and night, even after Karen returned. The neighbour called the cat Valentine, and thought a lot of her.

Karen started to wonder if she should take Sheba with her when she went to live in Switzerland (she had made the decision

Two of Karen's Entlebucher Mountain dogs, Barnabé (left) and Babiche (right)

that she was going to go), or if she should leave the cat with the neighbour. What would make Sheba happy?

The friend who had suggested telling Sheba how long her trips would be had another idea. She said for Karen to tell Sheba that if she wanted to go to Switzerland with her, that she had to come home every night to be with her. If she didn't come home in the evenings, Karen would know that the cat wanted to stay in California and "be Valentine."

Again, feeling a little silly, Karen relayed the message to Sheba. From that time onward, Sheba arrived home every single night. The message was clear. Sheba wanted to be with Karen.

When Karen moved to Switzerland in the mid-1980s, her life was very different from the one she'd experienced in the United States. The only constant in her life was Sheba. The cat was always there, ready to provide affection and comfort.

Then in 1990, Karen was walking along a beach when she saw a tall young man teaching a puppy how to swim. He seemed to know what he was doing; Karen thought that he understood animals. Little did she realize that he would soon become her husband!

> Again, feeling a little silly, Karen relayed the message to Sheba. From that time onward, Sheba arrived home every single night. The message was clear. Sheba wanted to be with Karen.

Two months after she met Jean-Marc on the beach with his pup, Barnabé, she moved to Quebec, Canada, with him to start a dairy farm.

Karen had had no previous experience with cattle. She found that when she entered the dairy barn, her mind was inundated with bits of conversation. She thought she might be going crazy. The cows couldn't really be talking to one another, could they?

One day, early in their dairy practice, Jean-Marc was worried about a cow that he thought should be pregnant, but she didn't appear to be. Karen heard words in her head: "false heat." She asked Jean-Marc what they meant. He looked at her curiously, wondering where she'd come up with the term. She said that she just heard the words in her head.

A friend of Karen's was a therapeutic riding instructor. Karen confided to her that she was hearing voices whenever she was in the barn. Her friend didn't suggest that Karen should seek psychological help, nor did she laugh at her; she told her about an animal communication course that was offered in New York State. Maybe Karen should check it out.

Karen decided to do that. She enrolled in a beginner course in telepathic animal communication at Spring Farm CARES with instructor Dawn Hayman, a follower of one of the pioneers of animal communication, Penelope Smith.

As she began the first session, Karen remembered thinking that if she was crazy, at least there was a whole roomful of other people there who were going through the same thing she was.

Spring Farm is home to a great variety of animals: horses, llamas, sheep, goats, ducks, dogs, cats. Dawn Hayman helped the members of the class find ways to reach out and connect with the animals, and to have some intent, some control, over the communication rather than simply receiving random messages.

Karen said of her first workshop with Dawn, "It was a very powerful class. I just remember feeling my mind—my spirit—really opening up and I didn't realize how much it had opened until after the class was over and I had a splitting headache, which Dawn told me it was very normal. She said [that happens] when you start using channels that you're not used to using in that kind of way. We were receiving information from all kinds of animals and Dawn would verify whether what we got was correct or...valid."

She returned to Spring Farm CARES twice to continue her animal communication training.

Karen found that being able to focus her listening abilities helped with the cows on the farm. At first, Jean-Marc was skeptical about what she was doing. But as she turned out to be right more often than not, he began to trust in her talents.

Karen's communication with the cows saved lives on the farm. One cow was due to give birth, but Jean-Marc wasn't sure just when to expect the calf. Karen told him the calf would arrive between one and two o'clock in the morning, it would be a difficult birth, and the baby would be a black bull calf.

Jean-Marc decided to go with Karen's "hunch" and set his alarm clock for one o'clock. When he entered the barn, the cow was in labour, and it was a breech birth. Jean-Marc was able to bring the calf into the world successfully, and indeed it was a black male.

Another time, a female calf became ill, and the vets could not find the source of the problem. Karen checked on the heifer and realized that she was in grave danger. She told Jean-Marc that if the calf didn't go to the hospital that night, she would be dead by morning. Karen was so sure, her husband loaded the calf into the van and took her to the vet hospital. That night, they operated on the calf for a disorder with its stomachs. Had they waited another day, the heifer wouldn't have survived.

Cows love to eat, and when one stops eating, it's a sign that something is not right. Karen remembers one time a cow that was soon due to calf would not eat, and the vet was at a loss to find the reason why. After the vet had left, Karen sat down in the barn in front of the cow and listened. One word came through to her: "Thirst." A cow who can't get water will not eat. Karen checked the water bowl. It wasn't working. They moved the cow to a stall where the water bowl worked, and after she'd had a good drink, she was hungry again.

In 1999, Jean-Marc and Karen made the decision to give up dairy farming. They knew that they wanted a nice quiet place to live. They explored many options. An intuitive told Karen to check out Nova Scotia. Jean-Marc and the children made a trip to the Maritimes, and really liked the area. Then Mary Stoffel, a friend who is also a holistic healer and animal communicator, told Karen she would settle in a place where rivers run into the sea and there was a grassy hill. That's just where they eventually found themselves—in Mahone Bay.

They left the cows behind, but they took the cats and their dogs with them to Nova Scotia. While on their farm in Quebec, and continuing when they moved to Nova Scotia, Karen raised a rare breed of Swiss herding dogs—the Entlebucher Mountain Dog. Jean-Marc's pup, Barnabé (the one that he'd been training to swim when he and Karen first met) was such a dog. In 1995, they got a female and they began to raise pups a year later.

The Entlebucher is a rare breed, but popular with those who know them. It is a black, tan, and white, medium-sized dog. It is powerfully built, energetic, affectionate, and intelligent.

Abby seemed to know her home as soon as she arrived there.

Karen has always felt that each of their pups has come into the world with a mission, and in order for them to accomplish their purpose in life, it's crucial that Karen not only finds each pup a good home, but that she finds it the *right* home. She looks for recognition between the pup and the prospective owner, or a vibration within herself that lets her know that this is a perfect match.

Karen recalls one pup who was born in their first litter. She placed her with a family from Connecticut. The adults in the family had, at one time, taken an animal communication course. Their previous dog had died, and they believed it would come back to them, reincarnated. Both the father and the daughter in the family believed their dog would return as an Entlebucher Mountain Dog, and they contacted Karen. Karen got the vibration that told her there was a strong connection with this family and she knew she would have a pup for them when the litter was born.

Through meditation Karen learned that the right pup for the Connecticut family would be the one who would be named Abby. Abby would be the largest female of the litter and she would make herself known to them.

The family did not want their pup's tail docked, as was the common practice. Tail docking is a form of cosmetic surgery that shortens a dog's tail. Since that procedure is carried out on the third day after birth, it would not give them much time to identify Abby.

Karen phoned the other people who had spoken for pups from this litter. When she explained that one buyer did not want the pup's tail docked, all the other buyers decided that they didn't want their pups' tails docked either. That took the pressure off recognizing Abby right off the bat.

The puppies finally arrived. The whelping pen was in the closet of Karen's bedroom. Karen had fallen asleep and was wakened by a noise. Only minutes after her birth, one pup had found a way out of the pen and was crawling across the bedroom floor! It was, of course, Abby.

Abby never bonded with her littermates. She held herself apart, as if waiting to go to her rightful place. When she was seven weeks old, the family from Connecticut took her home. They found that Abby knew their home as if she'd lived there her whole life. She recognized everything.

Not everyone who buys a puppy from Karen believes that there is a right dog for the right family. A fellow from Texas scoffed at such a notion. He decided he could pick any pup, and it would be fine. Karen laughed when she recalled that he'd pick up a pup and ask what its name was. "That's Gini." After he'd held Gini for a bit, he'd put her down, and then pick up a pup and ask its name. "That's Gini." Every time, he picked up the same pup! Needless to say, Gini was the dog he took home with him.

Karen feels that much of what she does is translation. She doesn't feel that animals necessarily think in words, the way we do. The messages she receives sometimes come to her as words and sometimes as awareness. She then has to interpret what was sent.

Animals are very spiritual beings, but like people, they have different levels of evolution of spirituality. Karen points out that there are master teachers as well as needy souls. An animal communicator should keep that in mind when receiving information.

Karen believes that if people invite the messages that animals are sending into their hearts and minds, they will hear them. The key is to sit and be quiet; to "stop and receive". When a person opens up to the communication, and trusts and accepts what is received, he or she has made a big step in animal communication.

Karen's son, Arlen, cuddles one of the pups.

Karen has an interest in someday providing a service for people who are grieving for a lost pet. She feels there is a lot she could offer that would bring comfort to them. At present, her challenge is to trust in what she is doing and put herself "out there" for the world to be aware of what she does.

Maggie, Calloway, and Karen all agree that anyone with the desire can learn to communicate with animals. Respect and openness are the keys that are necessary to begin.

EPILOGUE

Many people look at me like I have three heads when I tell them that I talk to animals. I have a dear niece who tells me that talking to animals isn't weird—it's believing that they talk back that is a little scary! However, experiences I've had with my animal companions lead me to trust in the gentle voices I hear.

Breezey Duchess was a border collie-cross and a very maternal soul. When we brought home tiny Tuxedo, a black and white kitten, she let him nuzzle her belly and knead her fur for comfort. The kitten often slept safe and warm on her back or on her front paws.

She used to keep all of our eight cats and four other dogs in line, doling out a disciplinary growl here, a lick for comfort there.

Breezey and I had a special bond. She often looked up into my eyes and we could practically hear one another's thoughts. One day I was planning to attend an animal communication workshop. Participants were permitted to take one animal along. I planned to take my big friendly dog, Casey. I knew he'd get along with everyone, human and animal.

Half an hour before I left for the workshop, Breezey sat by my chair and gazed up at me. I had no doubts that she was telling me she needed to go to the workshop, not Casey. So, she went. She caused a bit of trouble when she tried to steal the butter off the snack table (she was very food oriented!) but the facilitator chose her over the other animals present that day to practice with the participants. She connected with everyone and taught a great deal.

I later adopted Colbi, a husky-shepherd cross. The SPCA rescued him from a horrendous puppy mill. When I brought him home, he had never been in a house, never been handled by people, and he was blind. Despite being nearly starved, he seemed very gentle and trusting. I couldn't decide on a name for him at first, so I decided to sleep on it. That night, I dreamed that he spoke to me. He said, as clearly as could be, "My name is Colbi." I woke up with the name echoing in my head. I got up and said, "Come here, Colbi." This unsighted, untrained dog came right to me. He has been Colbi ever since.

Another remarkable dog was Casey. A butterscotch co-loured Lab-husky cross, Casey was the peacekeeper, the greeter, the caregiver. He knew that Colbi needed some special help. So he positioned Colbi right at his shoulder and he led him all around the house, showing him where things were. And when

Breezey and Casey

they went outside, Casey took him around the yard, steering him around swing sets and cars, between trees and along the driveway to the barn, until Colbi understood the layout. Once Colbi had gained some confidence and knew his way around, Casey felt he could leave his side. If he noticed Colbi becoming confused or lost, he would sidle up beside him, placing Colbi's nose at his shoulder, and he would lead him back to a familiar place.

Casey helped us out when another rescue dog, Brindle, a badly abused hound, came to stay with us. Little did we know when she arrived that she was a small Houdini. She escaped from her kennel shortly after she arrived, and she and Casey went for a romp on the marsh. I got home from work to find them a kilometer from home, running on the snow-covered fields. My husband and I went after them. I was terrified that Brindle would run off and we'd never find her.

Casey bounded up to us right away, looking for a biscuit and a scratch behind the ears. We fastened the leash on him. But Brindle was fearful and try as we might, we couldn't get close to her. After an hour, I decided to let Casey go again. I reasoned that he would head for home, looking for supper. Hopefully Brindle would follow him.

And then, the most incredible thing happened! When I unhooked the leash, Casey walked straight over to Brindle. He stood with her, nose to nose, for several seconds. Then he turned and walked straight back to me, with Brindle following him. She walked right up to me and stood stalk still while I clipped the leash on her. My husband and I were dumbfounded. Casey had clearly given Brindle the message to trust us and let us take her home.

As awesome as these events are, I think the day-to-day moments are even more special. They may not be as attention grabbing, but they plainly illustrate my companion animals' trust and caring.

When my white cat Flossy realizes I am ill, she curls up on me and purrs and purrs, giving me solace.

Colbi nudges his head under my elbow and cuddles against my side when I'm feeling blue. This is particularly wonderful since it took nearly a year before he welcomed any sort of human touch.

My skittish horse, Soti, was very careful to keep himself in balance and control when I rode him after I'd had an accident. He knew what I really needed was a very safe and quiet ride.

When I settle down to write with my laptop, our old cat Fudge insists on snuggling against my side, his chin resting on my arm or the edge of the keyboard. He is my inspiration and my greatest fan.

Animals are very sensitive beings with a great capacity for love and healing. It is tragic that many humans seem to have lost touch with the other creatures of this world. As the stories in this book show, there is so much to be gained by learning to connect, to trust and to communicate. In doing so, all our lives are enriched.

SOURCES AND RELATED READING

www.entlebucher.org

www.humanimal.com

www.mandalariding.com

www.maritimeanimalrescue.com

www.psanimal.com

www.purina.ca/about/halloffame

www.ravenshaven.petfinder.org

www.sja.ca/NSPEI/CommunityServices/
Programs/Pages/TherapyDogServices.
aspx

www.springfarmcares.org

www.therapyanimals.org

www.tlcshelter.com

PHOTO CREDITS

ACKNOWLEDGEMENTS

I would like to express my sincere thanks to all the wonderful animal lovers, trainers, and communicators who shared their stories with me. Many thanks to Wendy Knowlton, Olga Comeau, Nella Frosst, Marni Gent, Gail Rogerson, Eileen Turpin, Barbara Claussen, Marianne (Leblanc) Marshall, Christina Stevens, Dorothy Andrews, Wendy Cook, Dr. David Richardson, Nancy Noble, Jordan Noble, Corinne (Snow) Campbell, Kathleen Murphy, Colleen Archer, Elizabeth Archer, Corporal Rick Bushey, Maggie Carruthers, Calloway M'Cloud, and Karen Runge.

ABOUT THE AUTHOR

Joyce Grant-Smith was born in Annapolis Royal and has spent most of her life in the beautiful Annapolis Valley. She completed her BEd at Acadia University in 1979 and has enjoyed teaching in elementary and middle schools ever since. She and her husband, Les, have been married for over thirty years, and have raised two children, Jesse and Alexis, and a large menagerie of animals. Joyce's profound connection with some of her pets prompted her to learn more about animal communication.